Boundaries V for Kids

Fun, Educational & Age-Appropriate Lessons About Personal Safety & Consent |

Learn to Set Healthy Body Boundaries at Home, School, & Online

(For Ages 8-12)

By Barrett Huang

https://barretthuang.com/

© Copyright 2024 by Barrett Huang. All rights reserved.

This book contains information that is as accurate and reliable as possible. Regardless, purchasing this book constitutes an agreement that both the publisher and the author are in no way experts on the topics discussed and that any comments or suggestions made herein are solely for educational purposes. The information provided is not a substitute for professional medical advice, diagnosis, or treatment. Always consult a professional before taking any action advised herein.

This declaration is deemed fair and valid by both the American Bar Association and the Committee of Publishers Association and is legally binding throughout the United States.

Furthermore, the transmission, duplication, or reproduction of any of the following work, including specific information, will be considered illegal, whether done electronically or in print. This extends to creating a secondary or tertiary copy of the work or a recorded copy and is only allowed with express written consent from the publisher. All additional rights reserved.

The information in the following pages is broadly considered a truthful and accurate account of facts. Any inattention, use, or misuse of the information in question by the reader will render any resulting actions solely under their purview. There are no scenarios in which the publisher or author of this work can be deemed liable for any hardship or damages that may occur after undertaking the information described herein.

Additionally, the information in the following pages is intended only for informational purposes. It should thus be thought of as universal. It is presented without assurance regarding its prolonged validity or interim quality as befitting its nature. Trademarks mentioned are done without written consent and should not be considered an endorsement from the trademark holder.

FREE Guide: Mastering DBT Essentials

FREE DOWNLOAD ALERT!

Master Dialectical Behavior Therapy Skills in 5 Simple Steps with my Free DBT Quick Guide. Access the 'Mastering DBT Essentials' quick guide at:

https://barretthuang.com/dbt-quick-guide/

Or scan the code below:

Contents

FREE Guide: Mastering DBT Essentials 3
Contents 4
Introduction 6
   Dear Parents... 7
      How This Workbook Helps Your Child Learn about Boundaries 8
Understanding Boundaries 12
   What are Boundaries? 20
   Why are Boundaries Important? 22
Exploring Personal Space 26
   What Does Personal Space Mean? 39
   Defining Your Personal Space 42
   Exploring Different Personal Space Zones 46
Knowing Your Limits 50
   What Are Limits? 64
   Body Safety: Recognizing When You Feel Uncomfortable 71
      Good Touch vs. Bad Touch 71
      Safe Secrets vs. Unsafe Secrets 74
      Listening to Your Gut 74
Saying "No" 76
   What Does Saying "No" Mean? 82
   When Should You Say "No?" 82
   How to Say "No" 84
   Accepting "No" from Others 88
Exploring Your Boundary Universe! 90
   Family and Home Boundaries 102
      Sharing and Respecting Spaces and Belongings 102
      Balancing Time with Family and Friends 106
   Friends and Social Boundaries 111
   Feelings Boundaries 116

- Body Boundaries 120
- Time Boundaries 122
- Online Boundaries and Safety 126
  - Cyberbullying 131
  - Online Boundaries 132
- Self-Boundaries 134
- Firm, Fuzzy, and Shifting Boundaries 138
- Respect for Others' Boundaries 140
  - Reading Signs of Discomfort in Others 142
  - Learning to Ask for Permission 145
- Conclusion 146
- Bonus Section for Parents or Caregivers: How to Help Your Child Set Boundaries 148
- Review Request 151
- Further Reading 152
- About the Author 154
- References 155

Introduction

Hi there! 👋 How are you today? Please do me a favor and picture this in your amazing mind: Imagine that you're standing inside an invisible bubble or force field.

While standing inside this magical space, YOU get to decide who can come close, who should give you a little more space, and who should go away. That's right; you're the boss, and your bubble is the VIP, invitation-only section of your world!

Inside your bubble is your cozy personal space, where your feelings, ideas, thoughts, and body are extremely important. So, it's a bit like having your very own castle, and just like a castle has strong walls to keep out not-so-nice stuff, your *boundaries* are like the invisible walls that keep you safe and sound.

But guess what? Your bubble isn't just about keeping things out. It's also about letting good stuff in, like the warm hugs of your family, the high-fives of your friends, the feel-good words of others, and so on.

So, boundaries are not boring. If you think about it, it's actually a super power!

Boundaries are about having the power to say, "This is okay," or "I'm not comfortable with that," or "No." And you know what? It's 100% okay to have these feelings and say them.

And here's the magical part: everyone else has their own bubble, too! This means we all get to decide when to share our favorite toys, who to hang out with, when to have some quiet time and other stuff.

So, boundaries are also like magical maps where you can explore the land of friendships, family, school, and even adventures online. This map would guide you in making choices that feel right for you and show you how to treat others kindly.

So, gear up, boundary explorers! In the next pages, you'll be going on a fun and exciting exploration of boundaries with none other than **Tibby and Zip**—the world's favorite sibling kitties. 🐾

But before you go...

Remember, just like any skill, learning boundaries takes time and practice. And that's totally okay! You're already a champ because you're here and ready to learn and grow. So don't worry—you got this!

Dear Parents...

I know it can be hard to watch your child move further and further away from "home" and more and more "out there." This is why teaching your kids about boundaries is so important.

Boundaries are all about safety and protection. As such, the sooner they grasp the concept of boundaries, understand how to define their limits, and master the art of communicating them effectively to others, the better their interactions and relationships will be—now and in the future.

Of course, boundaries aren't just about physical space; they also encompass emotional and mental areas. In today's age, where online access and social media use by 8- to 12-year-olds are growing exponentially[1], teaching kids about the importance of online boundaries is critical to safeguard their well-being.

Further, learning about boundaries NOW lays the groundwork for setting healthy limits in the future. As they grow, your children will face numerous experiences and choices, some of which may be difficult to handle. However, suppose they possess a solid understanding of boundaries. In that case, they'll have the confidence to say "Yes" when the situation is aligned with their values and the strength to say "No" when needed.

Further, having a good sense of their limits helps them develop mental and emotional resilience. Kids are more likely to take care of themselves if they know their limits and have the power to stick to them. They'll know when they need a break, ask for help when they're having trouble, and how to develop a positive self-image.

By introducing the concept of boundaries in their formative years, you're cultivating a life skill that equips your children to become compassionate, confident, and respectful individuals. As they journey through various stages of life, they'll carry this knowledge like a guiding light, illuminating their path toward fulfilling relationships, personal growth, and a strong sense of self.

How This Workbook Helps Your Child Learn about Boundaries

Kids will learn about boundaries the FUN way because they'll be guided by Tibby and Zip, our resident sibling kitties. Each new chapter starts with a short story featuring Tibby and Zip to help kids learn distinct boundary concepts in a relatable manner. As they go along, plenty of activities and exercises are provided. This dynamic approach ensures that the invaluable lessons they've just read are reinforced and firmly grasped. So, let's get your kids started!

Worksheet: All About Me Backpack

Hello! This workbook has been specially created for you. So why don't you really put your stamp on it? You can use colors, pens, and crayons, draw and paste your picture—whatever suits you!

ALL ABOUT ME

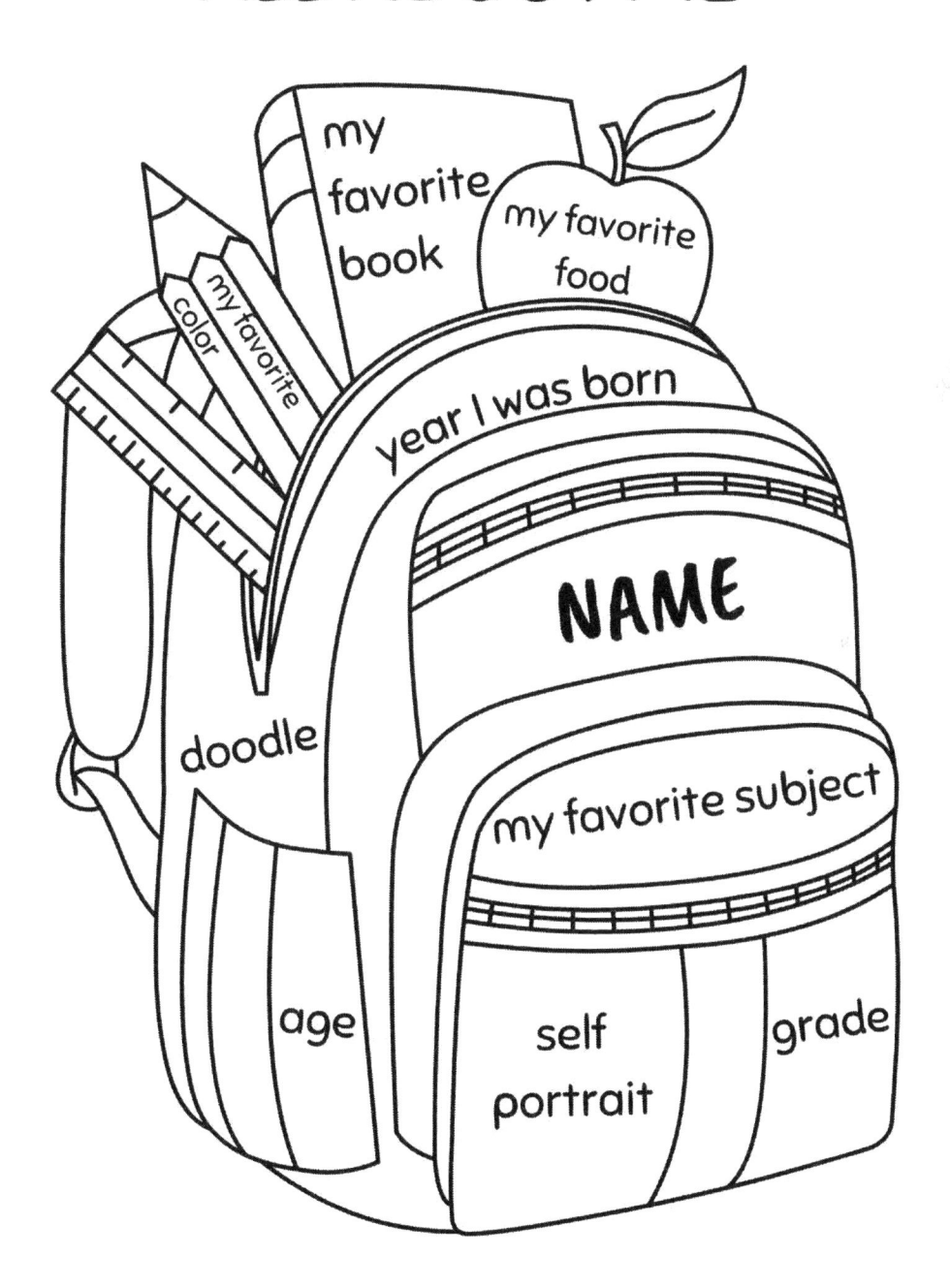

- my favorite book
- my favorite food
- my favorite color
- year I was born
- NAME
- doodle
- my favorite subject
- age
- self portrait
- grade

Worksheet: Safe Space Meditation

A "safe space" is like having a cozy corner of the world where you can be yourself without any worries. It's where you feel comfortable, happy, and free to express your thoughts and feelings. Ready to explore your safe space?

1. Find a quiet and comfy spot where you won't be disturbed. Close your eyes and take a deep breath.
2. Next, picture a magical place in your mind where you feel super safe and happy. It could be your bedroom, a cozy treehouse, or even a fluffy cloud in the sky! Take a moment to see all the colors, shapes, and details around you.
3. As you imagine your safe space, notice how it makes you feel. Are you warm and relaxed? Excited and happy? Let those good feelings fill you up.
4. Now, use your imagination to explore your safe space with all your senses. What does it smell like? Is there a gentle breeze or a soft touch? Can you hear birds singing or waves crashing? Feel the magic of your safe space all around you.
5. Next, how about you create a special spot within your safe space, like a comfy chair or a soft patch of grass. This is where you can sit or lie down and chill whenever needed. Imagine yourself there, feeling peaceful and content.

Remember, your safe space is always with you in your mind. It's a place you can go whenever you want to feel safe, calm, and happy. Take a deep breath, feel the good vibes, and slowly open your eyes when ready.

Great job! You've just created your very own safe space in your mind. You can visit this magical place anytime to relax or feel better.

Understanding Boundaries

Once upon a time, two adventurous sibling cats named Tibby and Zip lived in a cozy little neighborhood. They were known throughout the area for their curiosity and playful antics.

One summer morning, Tibby and Zip were walking down their street when Zip suddenly stopped in his tracks. Zip's eyes were round and super excited as he stared at a garden bursting with vibrant vegetables!

Just when Zip was about to scamper away into the vegetable garden, Tibby said, "Zip," her voice gentle but firm, "this is someone else's garden. We can't just go there and take their vegetables without asking. It's important to respect their space and their hard work."

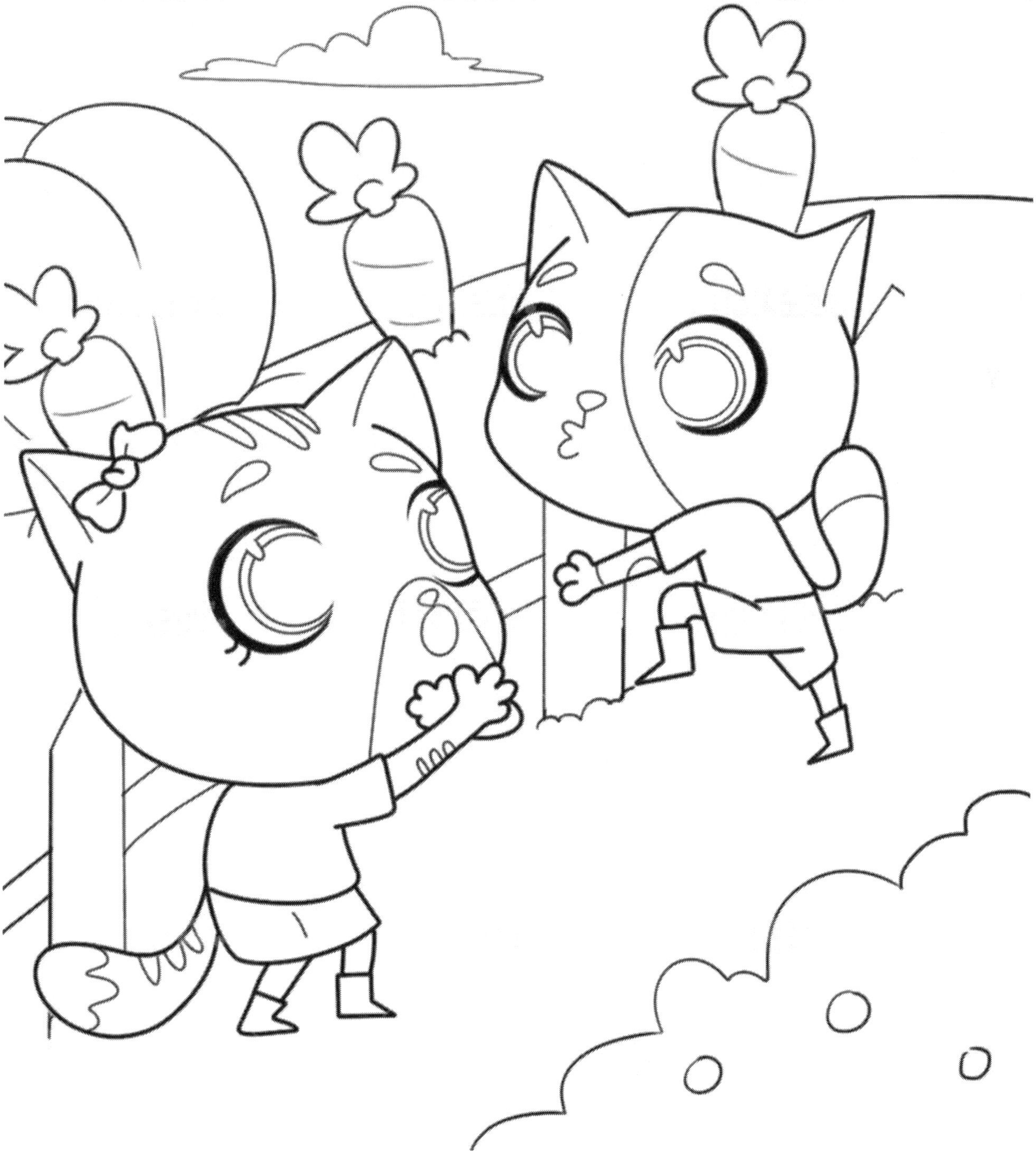

Zip: Why not? It's just out there, and all these veggies look so yummy!

Tibby: Zip, see this fence? That's called a **boundary**. It's like a little message that says, "This is our special area."

Look, even though it's not as big as this, we have our own little vegetable garden at home, and we can enjoy the vegetables there. And if we want something from someone else's garden, we should ALWAYS ask first. You don't want anyone just taking one of your toys, do you?

Zip: No, I don't like other cats taking my toys! You're right, Tibby. I guess I just got carried away when I saw all these tasty treats! Let's go home.

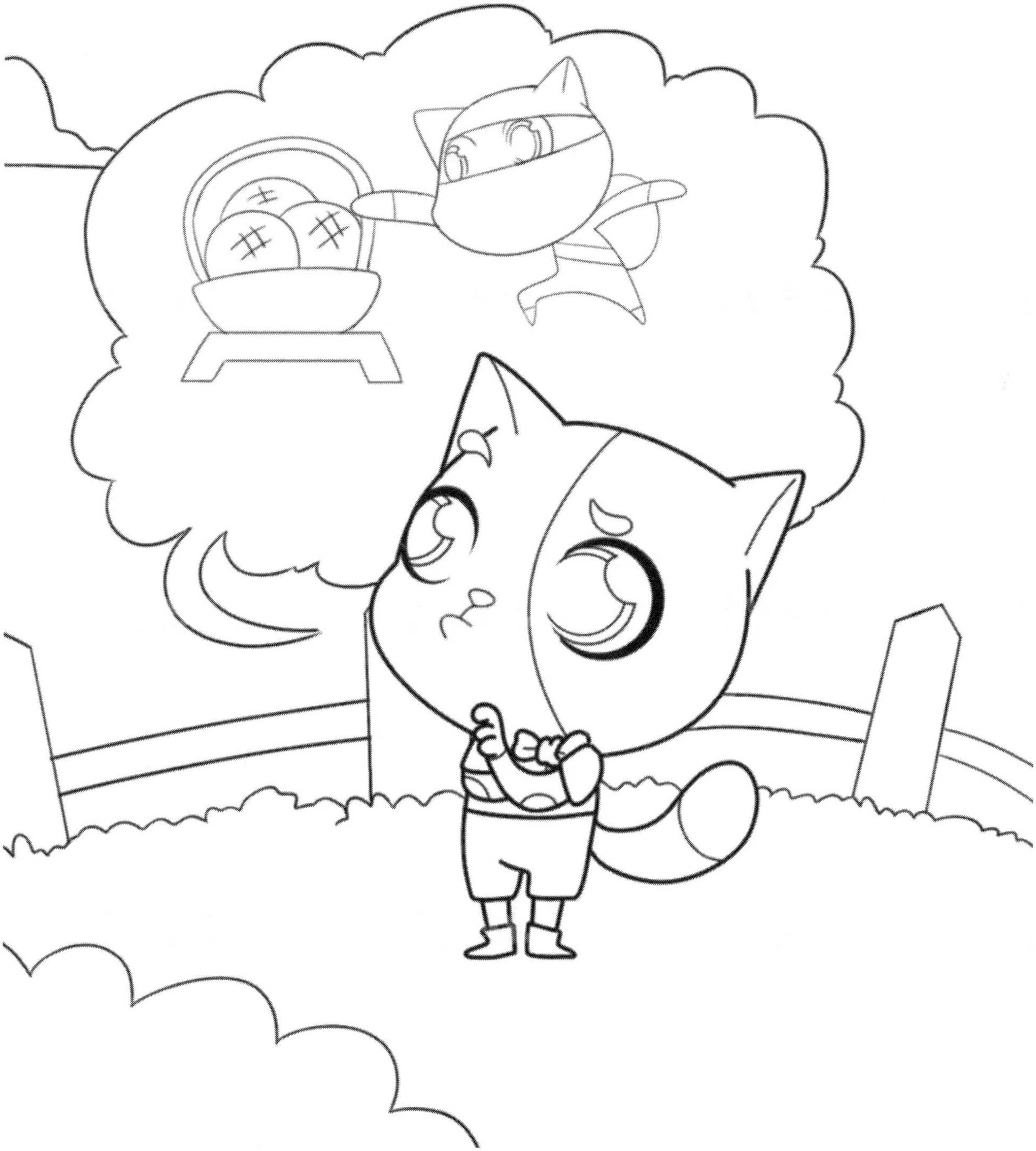

What are Boundaries?

A boundary is like an invisible fence showing where your space starts and ends. They help you feel comfortable and safe because it's like a magic rule that tells people how close they can come to you and how you want to be treated. Boundaries help you decide who can give you a high-five, a hug, a kiss on your cheek, or a pat on the back.

Boundaries are not the same for all people in your life. For example, when it comes to your parents, you're probably okay with them giving you a tight hug. However, if a kid you just met at school tries to do that, that's not cool, right?

It's also important to note that your boundaries may change as your friendships and relationships change. For example, on Day 1 of school, you might not be okay with a new friend giving you a tight hug. But suppose you two become besties over the school year? Maybe then, you'll be comfortable with tight hugs from them. And if not, that's okay, too.

You see, that's the cool thing about boundaries. YOU determine what they are for you.

It's super-duper important to know that boundaries are not always the same as not liking something. For example, you might like or even hate broccoli, but that doesn't mean it's a boundary. Boundaries are more about your feelings about what is right and wrong for you. They help you express how you want to be treated and what makes you feel safe and happy. So, not liking broccoli is a personal preference; it has nothing to do with your feelings of safety, comfort, and security.

Worksheet: Exploring Your Boundary Bubble

Imagine standing inside an invisible boundary bubble. You feel safe and comfortable here. Now, let's explore what you like and don't like.

What things do you like? These are things that can come inside your bubble. *Example: your fav sweater, your oldest toy, your fav food, etc.*

_____
_____
_____
_____

Who are the people you like and trust? These are people who can visit inside your bubble. *Example: your parents, your baby sister, your grandma, etc.*

_____
_____
_____
_____

What should be outside your bubble? These things or situations make you uncomfortable, sad, or even mad. You don't want these inside your bubble. *Examples: loud noises, my brother using my laptop without asking, my classmate tasting my lunch*

_____
_____
_____
_____

Why are Boundaries Important?

All this talk about boundaries... do you really need it? Yes, you do! They're very important for many reasons:

1. **Safety**. Boundaries help keep you safe, ensuring everyone respects your personal space and feelings.

2. **Self-respect.** When you learn about boundaries, you get to understand yourself better. You learn about your feelings and limits, which help you respect yourself.

3. **Respect for others.** Every single person on this planet has boundaries. And setting and following boundaries teaches you to think about how others feel, too, so you can treat everyone kindly.

4. **Healthy self-image**. Knowing your boundaries helps you understand who you are and what you like, making you feel good about yourself.

5. **Healthy relationships.** Understanding boundaries helps you make good friendships that respect each other's space and feelings.

6. **Confidence**. You feel strong and confident about yourself when you set boundaries and stand up for them!

7. **Independence**. Boundaries let you make decisions for yourself, which is an important part of growing up.

8. **Less stress.** When you have clear boundaries, you know what to expect, making you feel more in control of situations and less stressed.

9. **Better communication skills.** Boundaries are not supposed to be secrets. Once you identify your boundaries, you need to be able to express them in a kind but firm way, especially when someone is crossing them. This improves your communication skills!

10. **Preventing overwhelm.** Setting boundaries helps you avoid taking on too much at once so you don't get overwhelmed.

11. **Conflict resolution.** Boundaries provide a lot of clarity about how you and others want to be treated. When boundaries are clear and respected, you'll be better at preventing and solving problems when they arise.

12. **Digital well-being.** In the digital world, boundaries help you know how much screen time is good and how to stay safe online.

13. **Building character.** Following boundaries helps you build important qualities like being patient and doing the right thing.

14. **Emotional regulation**. Boundaries help you understand and manage your feelings to feel happier inside.

15. **Preventing exploitation.** Boundaries protect you from things that might be unsafe and people who might not want the best for you. They prevent you from being used, taken for granted or exploited.

You see? Boundaries are very important! They're like superhero powers to keep you safe, happy, and confident in all sorts of situations.

Worksheet: Wordsearch

Can you find the boundaries-related words in this puzzle?

Words can be found in any direction (including diagonals). Use the word bank on the right to know which words to find.

Boundaries Wordsearch

Y	C	O	M	M	U	N	I	C	A	T	I	O	N
G	T	S	J	I	P	R	B	X	Q	A	G	B	T
G	R	K	L	N	C	R	E	E	K	D	J	W	D
Q	U	K	B	D	C	R	I	S	O	W	W	O	O
P	S	C	O	E	O	F	G	V	P	Y	I	N	V
E	T	O	U	P	M	E	R	E	A	E	I	T	E
R	C	N	N	E	F	E	O	M	U	C	C	X	R
S	O	F	D	N	O	L	A	O	X	R	Y	T	W
O	N	I	A	D	R	I	C	T	X	S	S	U	H
N	F	D	R	E	T	N	X	I	M	A	T	C	E
A	L	E	I	N	A	G	B	O	G	F	R	O	L
L	I	N	E	C	B	S	M	N	S	E	E	Q	M
R	C	C	S	E	L	T	Q	S	J	T	S	E	C
N	T	E	Q	T	E	I	H	J	E	Y	S	S	X

RESPECT
BOUNDARIES
PRIVACY
SAFETY
PERSONAL
INDEPENDENCE
CONFIDENCE
COMMUNICATION
CONFLICT
OVERWHELM
STRESS
COMFORTABLE
FEELINGS
EMOTIONS
TRUST

Exploring Personal Space

Tibby loves having her own room where she can relax and re-energize. Every day, Tibby would arrange her toys and make a cozy spot in her room where she could curl up and enjoy some alone time.

But no matter how many times she reminds
Zip NOT to enter her room without knocking,
he always does it anyway!

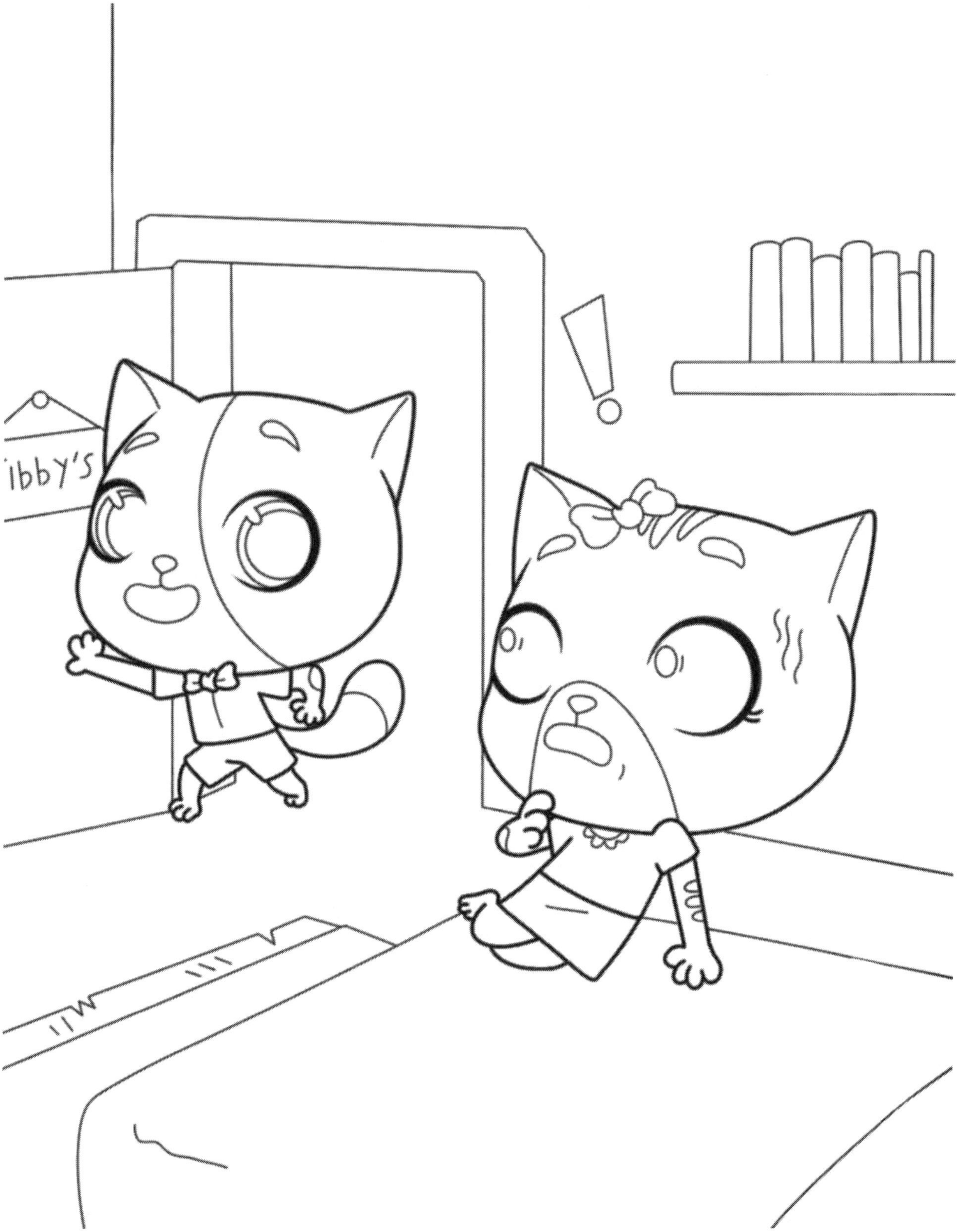
ibby's

30

So, one bright morning, Tibby thought it was time to take care of the issue. With a serious look on her face, she called Zip into her room. "Zip," she said softly, "I want to talk to you about boundaries and personal space. My room is my private place, and you shouldn't just come in when you want to."

Zip's wide, innocent eyes blinked, and he tilted his head. He didn't fully understand the idea of "boundaries" and "personal space."

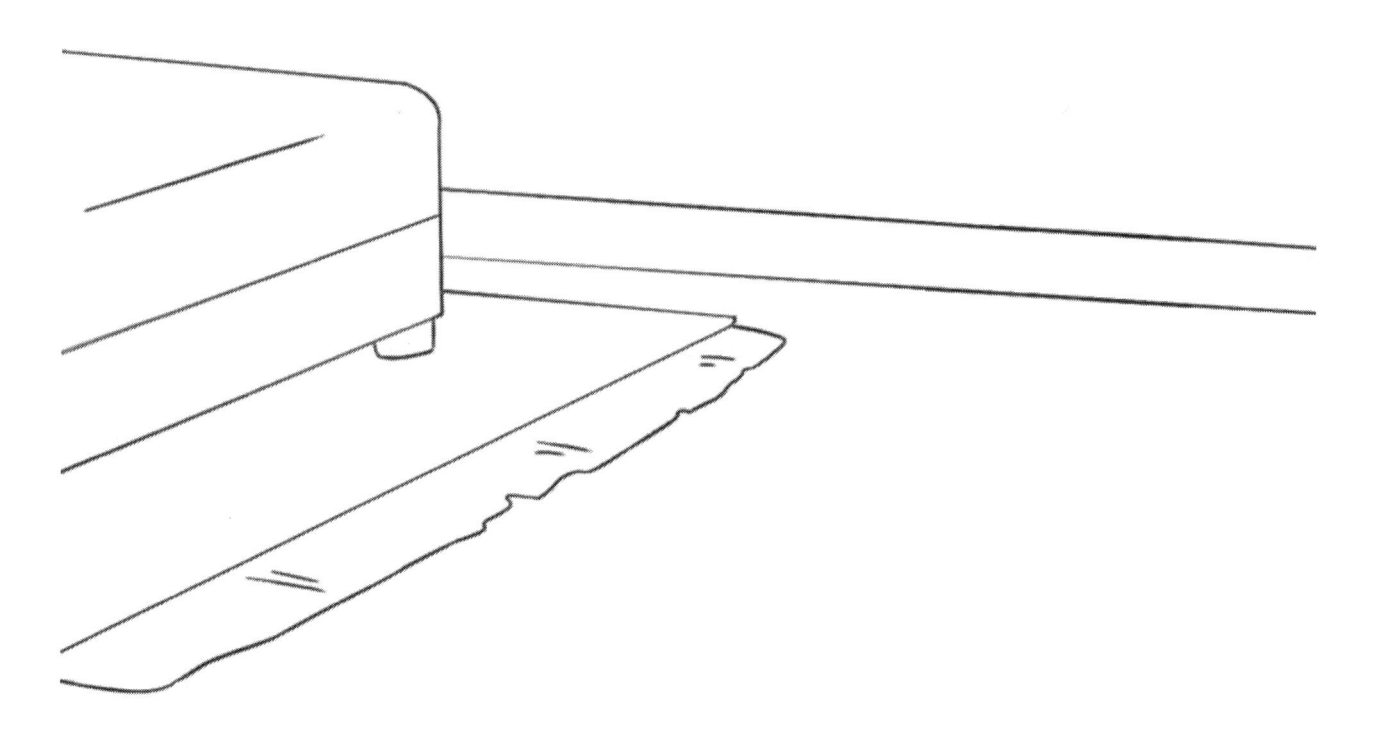

Tibby said, "You see, Zip, this whole room is my personal space. Now, imagine my door as my boundary. It means that's where my personal space starts."

Tibby's

33

True to his word, whenever Zip wanted to go into Tibby's room, he would stop and think about what they had discussed.

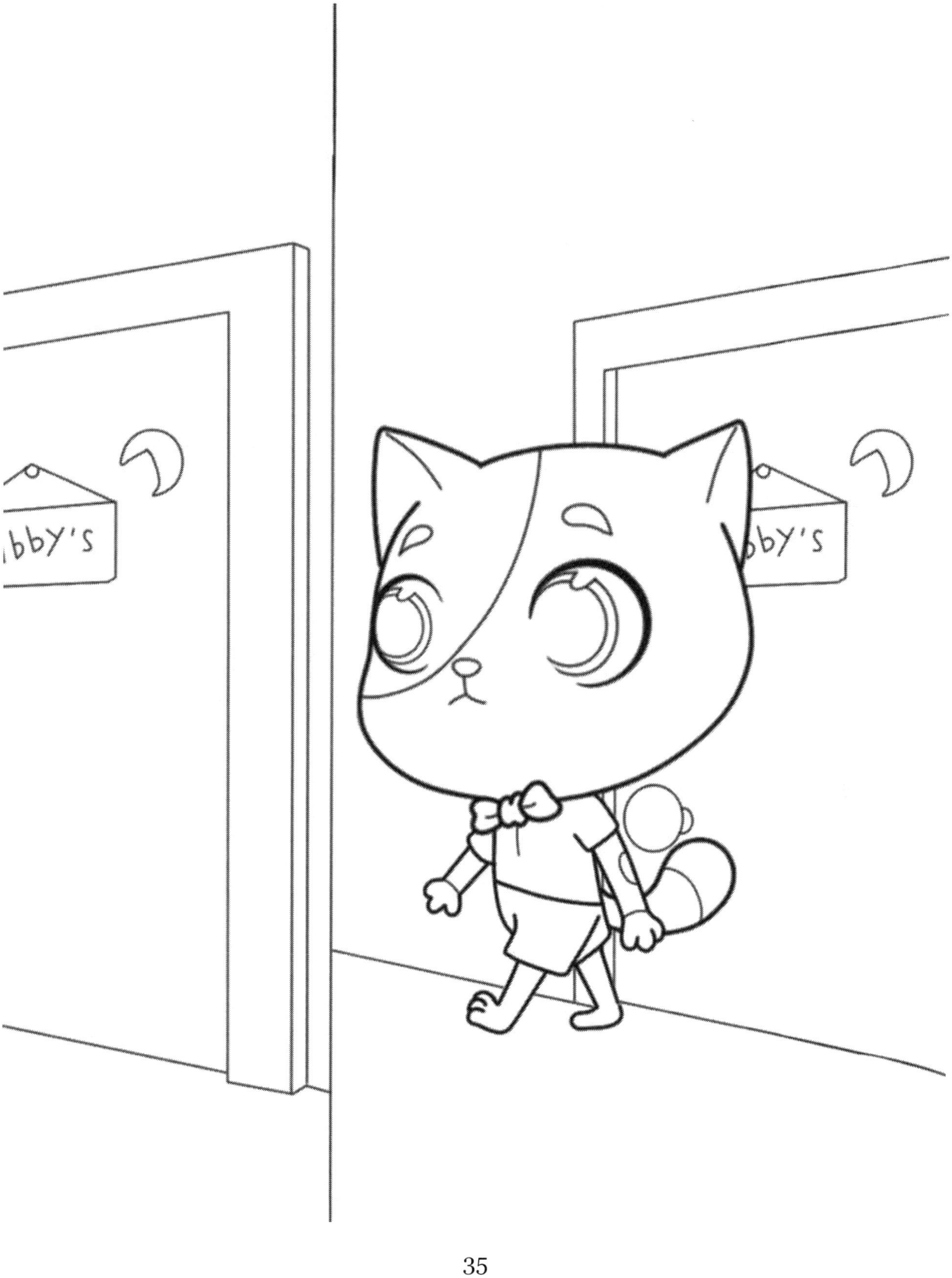
bby's
bby's

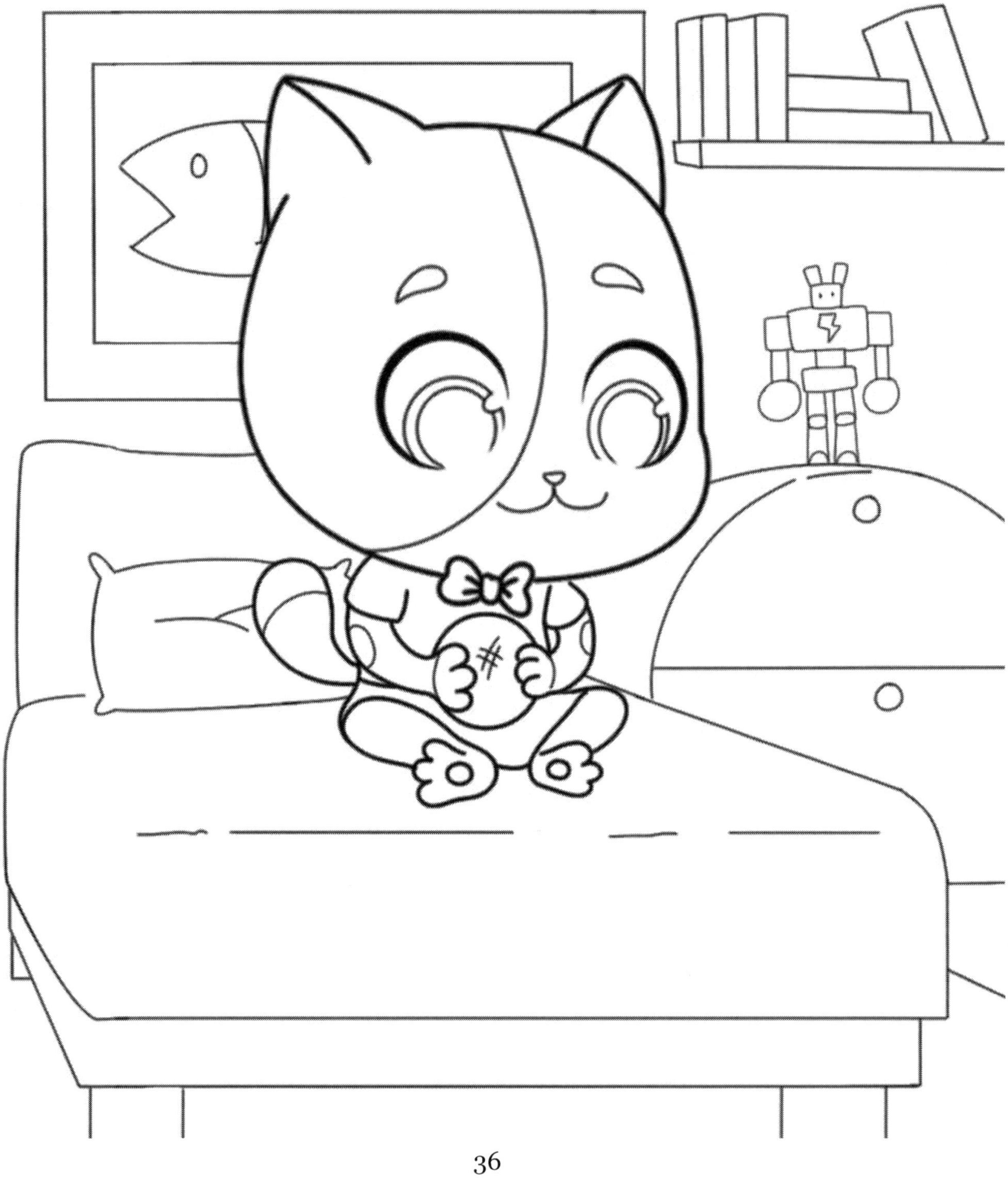

Tibby appreciated that Zip remembered their talk about boundaries and started to invite him to her room a few times. They'd cuddle up together and tell each other stories or play with their toys. Tibby also showed Zip how to make his own relaxing place in another part of the house!

Quiz Time: Personal Space Boundaries

Quick! Get your favorite pencil, pen, or color marker. Answer the following questions based on the story you read about Tibby and Zip and respecting personal space boundaries.

1. **What are boundaries?**
    a.) Invisible lines that keep siblings apart.
    b.) Invisible lines that should always be crossed.
    c.) Invisible lines that protect personal space and belongings.

2. **Why did Tibby feel upset when Zip entered her room without permission?**
    a.) Tibby didn't like playing with Zip.
    b.) Tibby wanted to have her own space and relax.
    c.) Tibby didn't want Zip to find her toys.

3. **How did Tibby and Zip resolve the issue of entering Tibby's room without permission?**
    a.) Tibby locked her room to keep Zip out.
    b.) Tibby and Zip discussed boundaries and agreed to respect each other's personal space.
    c.) Tibby gave all her toys to Zip so he could play on his own.

4. **What did Zip learn about boundaries?**
    a.) Boundaries are meant to keep siblings apart.
    b.) Boundaries can be ignored.
    c.) Boundaries are important for respecting personal space and belongings.

5. **Why is it important to respect each other's boundaries?**
    a.) To make the other person feel upset.
    b.) To create a harmonious and respectful environment.
    c.) To have more toys to play with.

Great job! You've successfully completed the quiz. How did you do? Check your answers with a trusted adult!

What Does Personal Space Mean?

Do you remember your magical, invisible bubble?

This bubble is your personal space. It's the area around you where you feel comfortable and safe. Just like you wouldn't want someone too close to you when you're eating or playing, personal space gives you enough room to feel good. It's like having your own invisible zone; only you get to decide who can join you.

Boundaries, however, are like the rules you make for your bubble. They help you decide how you want to be treated and what's okay or not in your bubble.

So, personal space is your special zone, and boundaries are the rules that keep it just how you like it!

Worksheet: Personal Space Circle

Imagine this: you're in your personal space. Now, WHO are the people who can stand close to you? WHO can touch your shoulder?

The example below shows that Adam feels safest and most comfortable with his immediate family. After them, he feels closest to his grandparents and Uncle Jimmy. After that, he feels somewhat close or at least comfortable with some of his teachers and coaches and even Mr. Dave next door, and so on.

Important: YOU are the only person who should be in your personal space. Sometimes, people in the next circle (e.g., family) can enter your personal space for a kiss or a hug, but ONLY if it's okay with you.

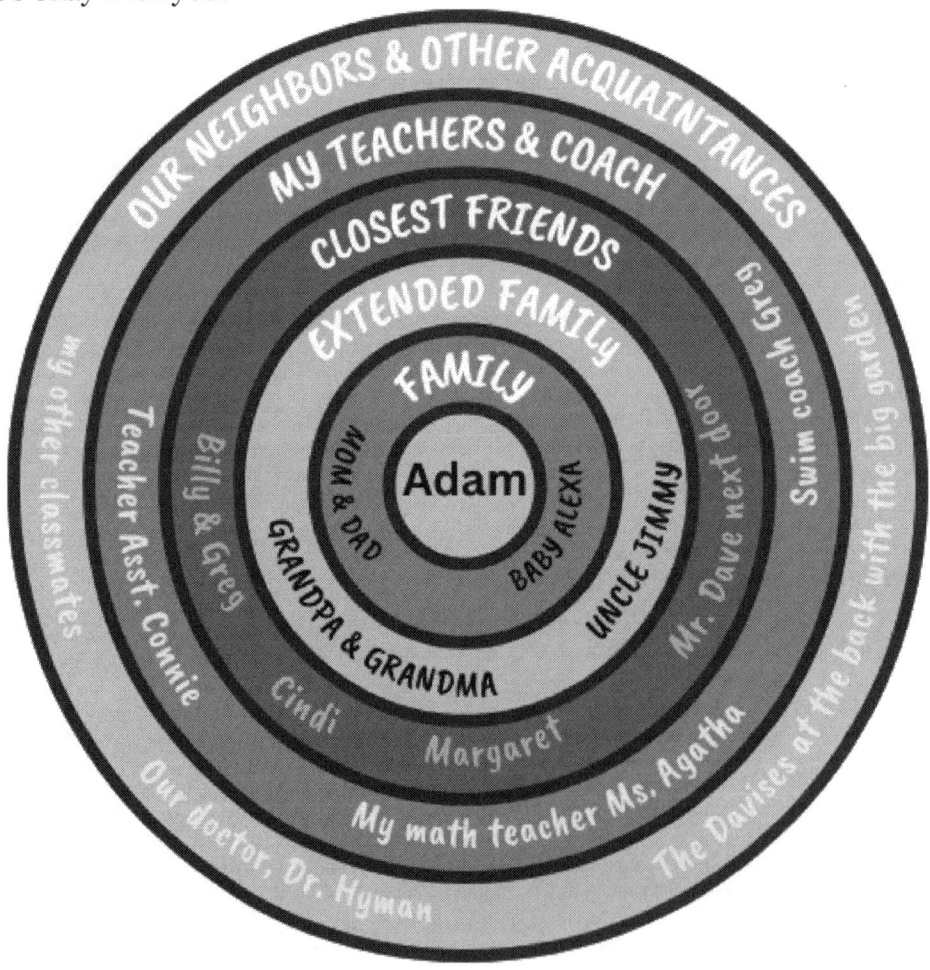

Now, it's your turn!

Fill out the circle below with the people or groups of people you feel safe and comfortable with. Remember, there is no right or wrong answer. That's because personal space is different for everyone. So, just write down what feels good in your heart.

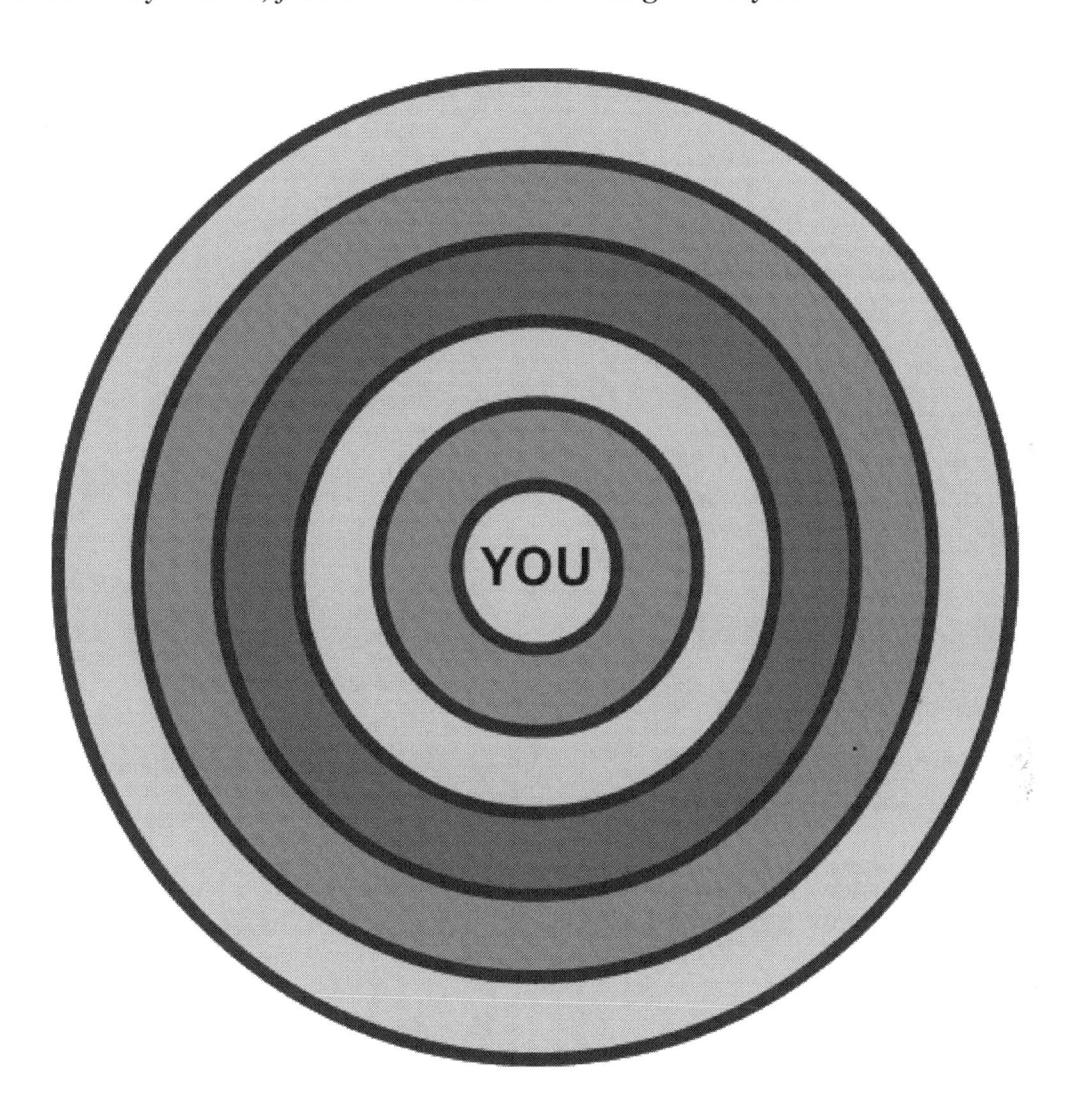

Defining Your Personal Space

In the last activity, you wrote down the closest people to you. But that doesn't mean they must follow the same rules or boundaries.

For example, Mom and Dad can come into your personal space for a kiss and a hug, but you're only okay with a hug (no kissing) from your grandparents or uncles and aunts. Sometimes, when you're upset, you might not want a kiss from Mom and Dad but only a hug. Is that confusing? Here are some things to think about:

1. **Think about your happiness and comfort.** What makes you feel comfortable and happy when you're around people? Do you like it when they're close or prefer more space?

    For example, you might be super okay with Mom and Dad sitting next to you on the sofa with an arm over your shoulders. Still, you probably won't like it if someone else did that, right?

2. **Imagine your bubble.** Picture that invisible bubble around you again. If someone enters your bubble, how close can they be before it feels "too much?"

3. **Physical activities with friends.** When you're playing games or hanging out with friends, how close can they be to you? Is there a distance that feels "just right" for you?

4. **Hugs and high-fives.** Do you like hugs, high-fives, or handshakes? How do you feel about people giving you a pat on the back?

I'm okay with:	From:
Example: ✓ Hugs	*Example:* *Mom and Dad, my sister, Grandma and Grandpa, Uncle Jimmy*
☐ Hugs	
☐ High-fives	
☐ Handshakes	
☐ Pat on the back	

5. **Your feelings.** Think about times when someone got too close. How did that make you feel? *Example: I felt really uncomfortable. I wanted to squirm away.*

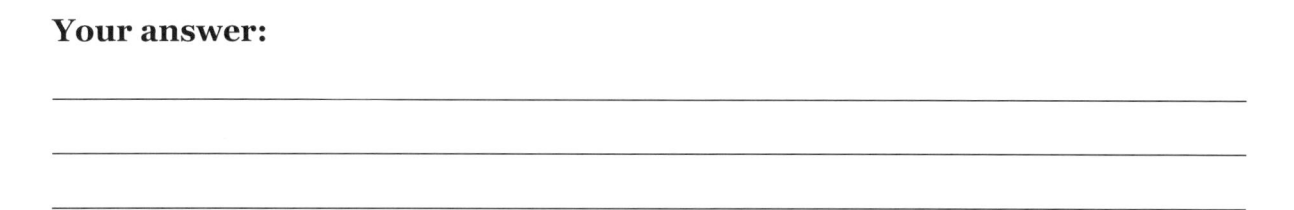

Your answer:

_____

_____

_____

Still not sure about the rules concerning your personal space? That's okay. Consider yourself as a "personal space explorer" for now. And as such, you might not have all the answers yet. To help you, here are two little experiments!

Experiment A: Chicken Wings

Put your hands on your hips. Someone's too close to you (or you're too close to someone) if your elbow touches them when your arms are spread out like chicken wings.

Experiment B: Personal Space Detective

Try standing in different spots and see how close someone can get before you feel like you need more space. This can help you figure out your rules about personal space with that specific person.

Worksheet: My Personal Space Rules

Personal space is a lot about "distance," but that can mean many things, too. For example, you might be okay with your best friend sitting or standing super-duper close to you, but you don't like it when they touch your hair or take food from your plate during lunch.

We often get into misunderstandings or fights with others because we're unsure about our personal space boundaries. So, how about we dive into that?

In the tables below, write **what's okay** and **what's not okay** for the groups of people below. (Use more sheets of paper if you have to!)

IMMEDIATE FAMILY (Mom, Dad, brothers, and sisters.)	
Okay 👍	Not Okay 👎
Example: tight hugs	*Example: kissing me on the lips in public!*

EXTENDED FAMILY (Grandparents, uncles, aunts, etc.)	
Okay 👍	Not Okay 👎
Example: hugs	*Example: making me sit on their laps. I'm too old for that!*

FRIENDS & CLASSMATES	
Okay 👍	**Not Okay** 👎
Example: walking hand-in-hand or arms linked	*Example: kissing my cheek*

TEACHERS & COACHES	
Okay 👍	**Not Okay** 👎
Example: handshakes	*Example: hugs*

NEIGHBORS	
Okay 👍	**Not Okay** 👎
Example: fist-bumps, high-fives	*Example: standing too close*

Exploring Different Personal Space Zones

You're always inside your personal space bubble. But bubbles are not fixed sizes. Sometimes, they can become smaller or expand; this all depends on who you're with and where you are. Yep, personal space zones can be all mysterious and stuff!

Home

Imagine your home as a big puzzle; each room is a puzzle piece. As you move around, each room has different personal space zones.

You might want more personal space in your bedroom when studying, reading a book, or playing quietly. It's your cozy retreat where you feel super comfortable.

Your personal space might be a bit smaller in the living room because it's where the family gathers. You still have your invisible bubble, but it might be smaller around you as you get close to others when watching a movie or playing a game.

School

Just like you have different personal space zones at home, you also have unique ones at school.

Your personal space is like an invisible circle around your desk in the classroom. It's where you feel comfortable when working on your assignments or listening to the teacher. If someone's desk is too close to yours, it might feel crowded.

During recess, your personal space might change. When you're playing a game like tag, you might be okay with friends being closer to you as you run around. But if you're sitting and reading a book, you might want a bit more space to enjoy your story.

Lunchtime is another interesting example. You might share a lunch table with friends, and that's okay because you're all sitting together. But if someone's seated super close and you need more space, it's totally fine to ask for some room kindly.

Mall

Like at home and school, you also have unique personal space zones at the mall. You might want more room to move around in stores when browsing shelves for cool stuff.

Waiting in line is another great example. Your personal space in line is the distance you feel comfortable standing behind the person in front of you. It's like ensuring you have enough room to breathe and be patient.

Your personal space might change at the food court, depending on what you're doing. If you're eating, you might want your space to enjoy your meal. But if you're chatting with friends, your bubble might be a bit closer because you're all conversing.

Other Places:

If you're visiting a close friend's home, your personal space bubble might be smaller because you know the people in that house. So you might be okay if they're standing or sitting close to you.

However, your personal space bubble expands if you're somewhere you're not familiar with. For example, suppose it's your first time at a new friend's home, and you get introduced to their parents. In this case, be polite and give your greetings, but if you're not okay with them standing close, patting you, or touching your shoulder, then it's perfectly fine to move away and keep your distance.

Playing Sports:

Personal space is just as important on the field or court as anywhere else.

Imagine you're playing soccer. Your personal space is like an invisible area around you that helps you control the ball and move around. If someone gets too close, it might be harder to kick the ball. So, you create a bubble that gives you enough room to play your best.

In basketball, personal space matters, too. When guarding a player, you want to be close enough to defend but not so close that they can easily pass you. It's all about finding the right balance to be effective while respecting their space.

If you're into swimming, it doesn't matter if you're fast or slow. What matters is that your personal space is not invaded. So, if you don't like someone swimming too close to you, move out of the way. If they keep doing it, tell them or inform an adult.

Remember, your personal space bubble is ALWAYS around you. It may change its shape or become smaller or bigger depending on the people around you and where you are, but it's always there, and it should always be respected.

Knowing Your Limits

It's bedtime for Tibby and Zip!

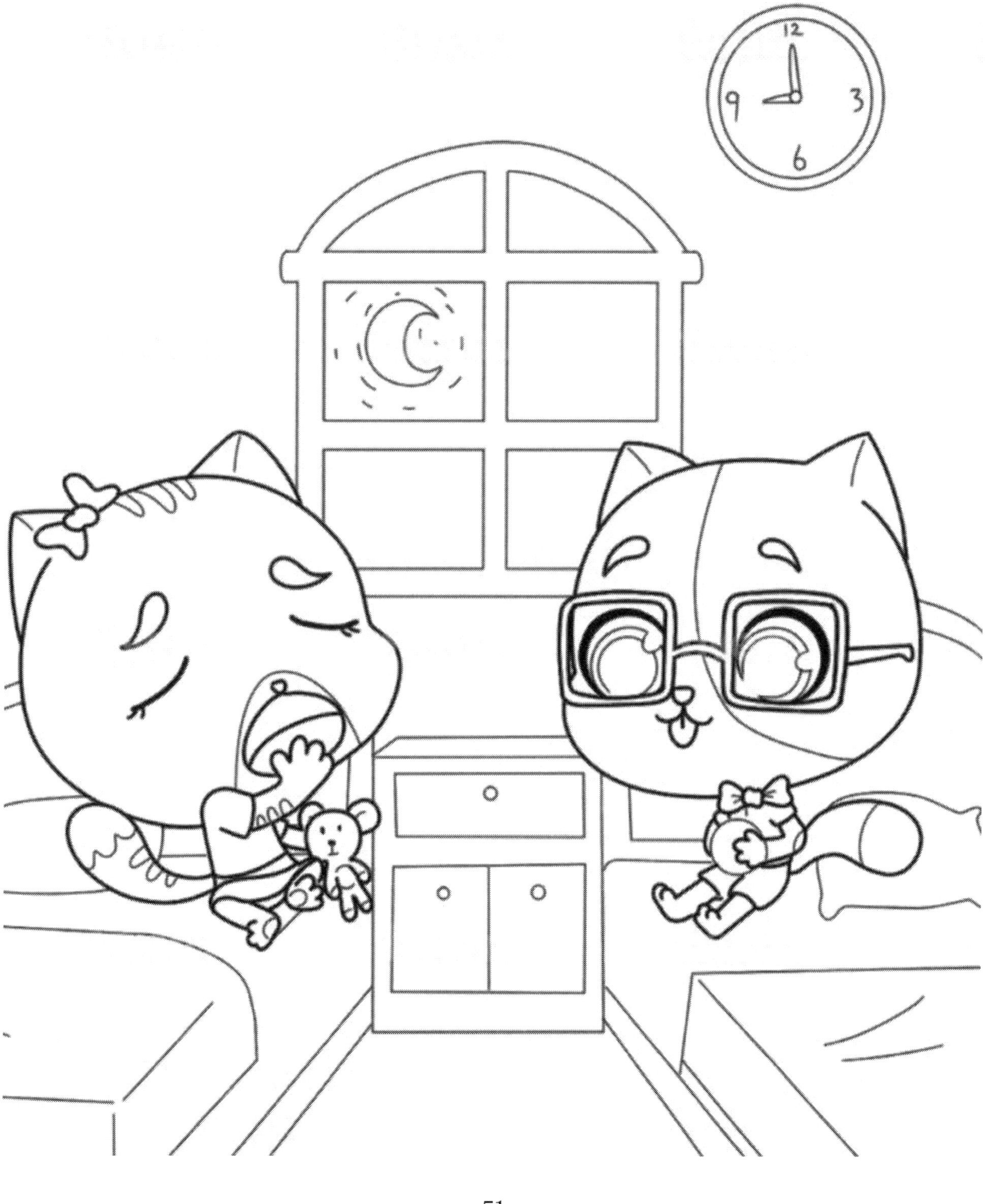

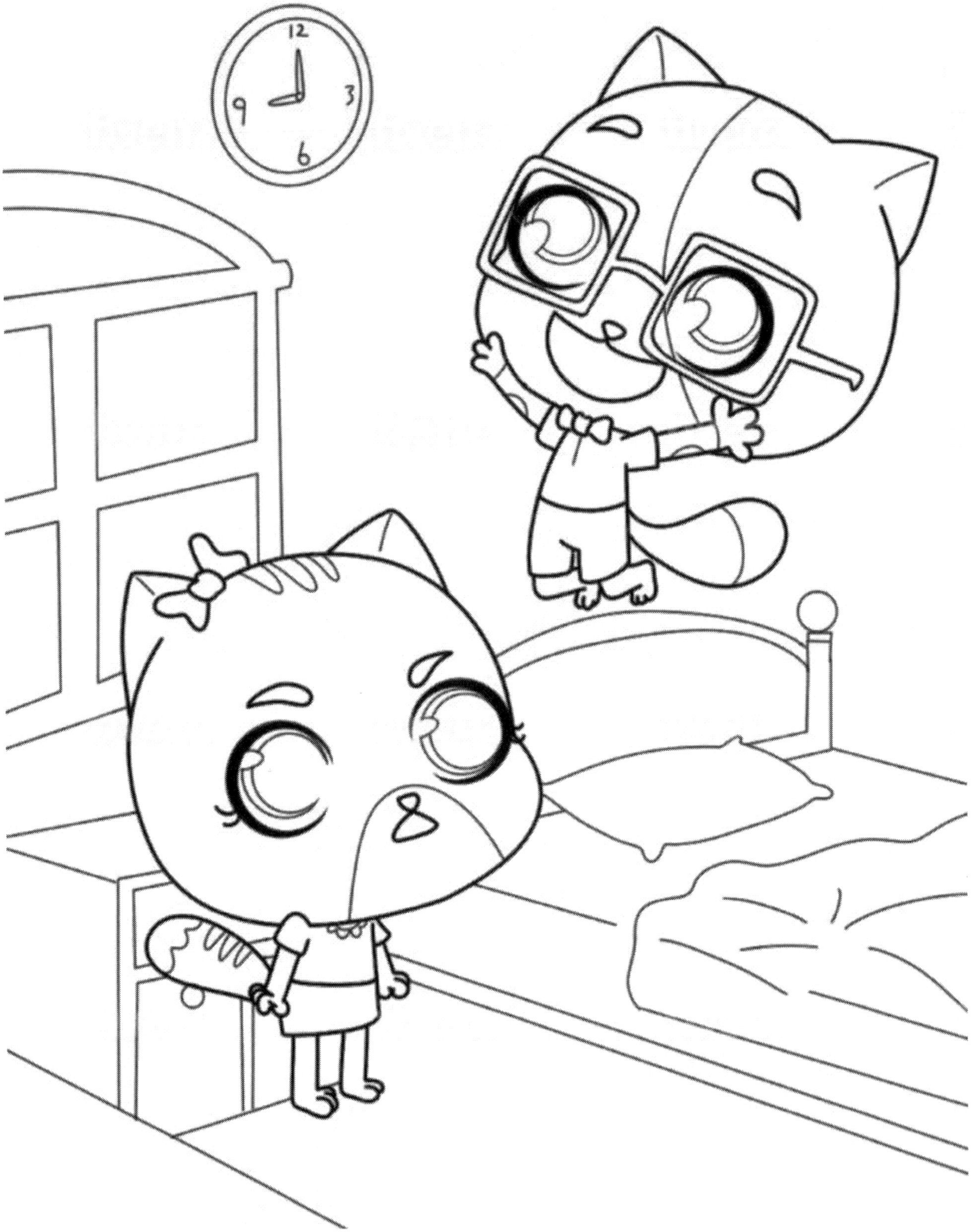
12
3
9
6

Tibby: Zip! It's time to sleep.
Zip: Sleep is for the weary! I'm not weary!

Tibby: Sleep is NOT for the weary Zip.
Sleep is for adventures into dreamland.
Zip: Yeah, right!

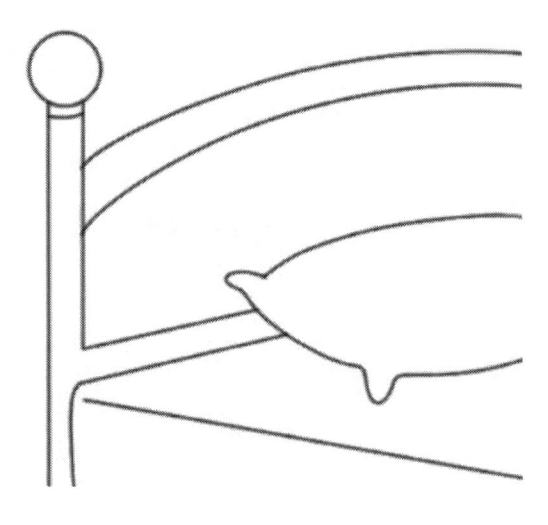

55

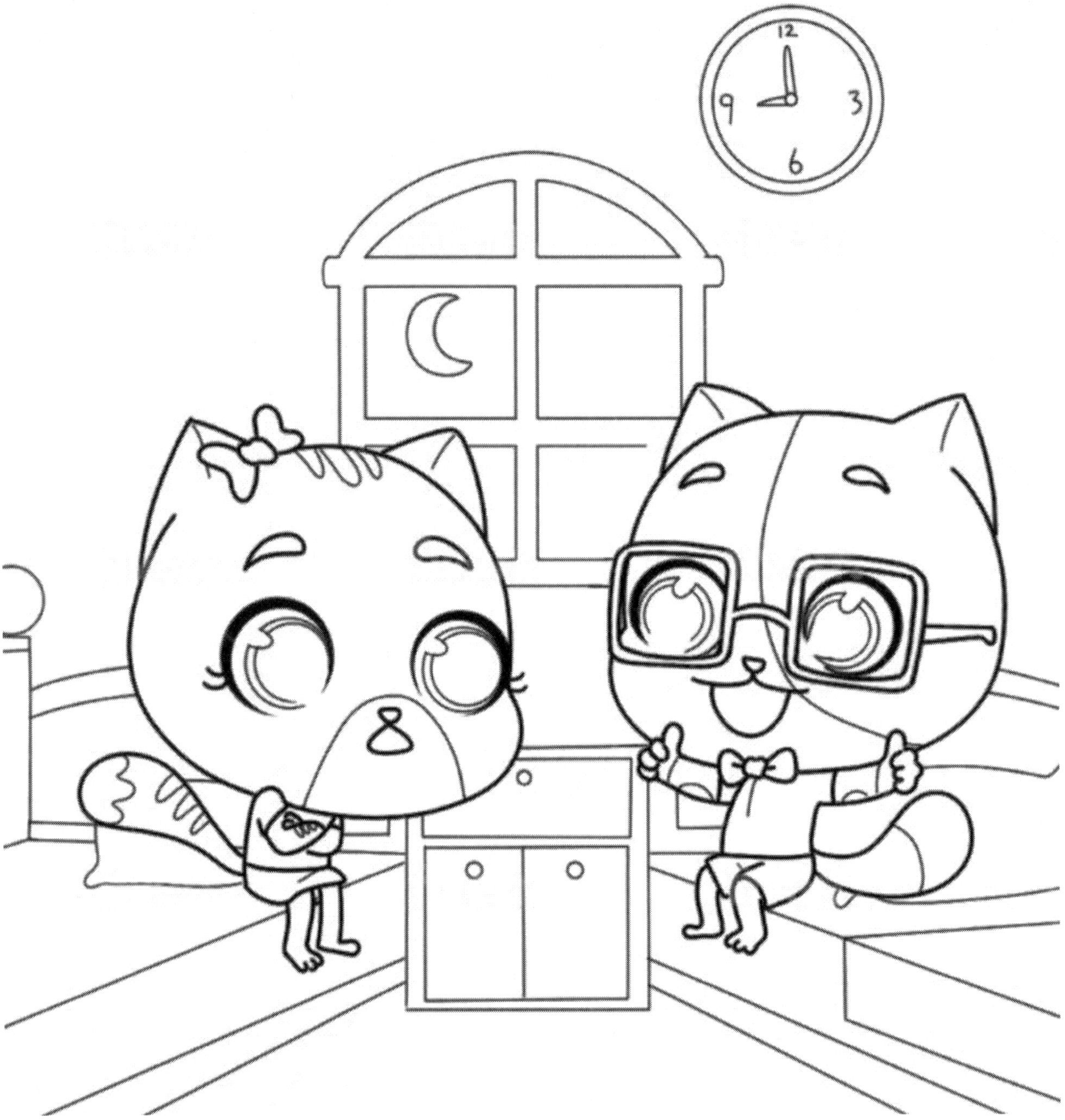
12
3
6
9

Tibby: Alright, how about we make a deal, Zip? I'll sleep, and you can stay up. But tomorrow, you still need to get up at the same time as usual and do your chores.
Zip: Deal!

And so Zip played and played all night...

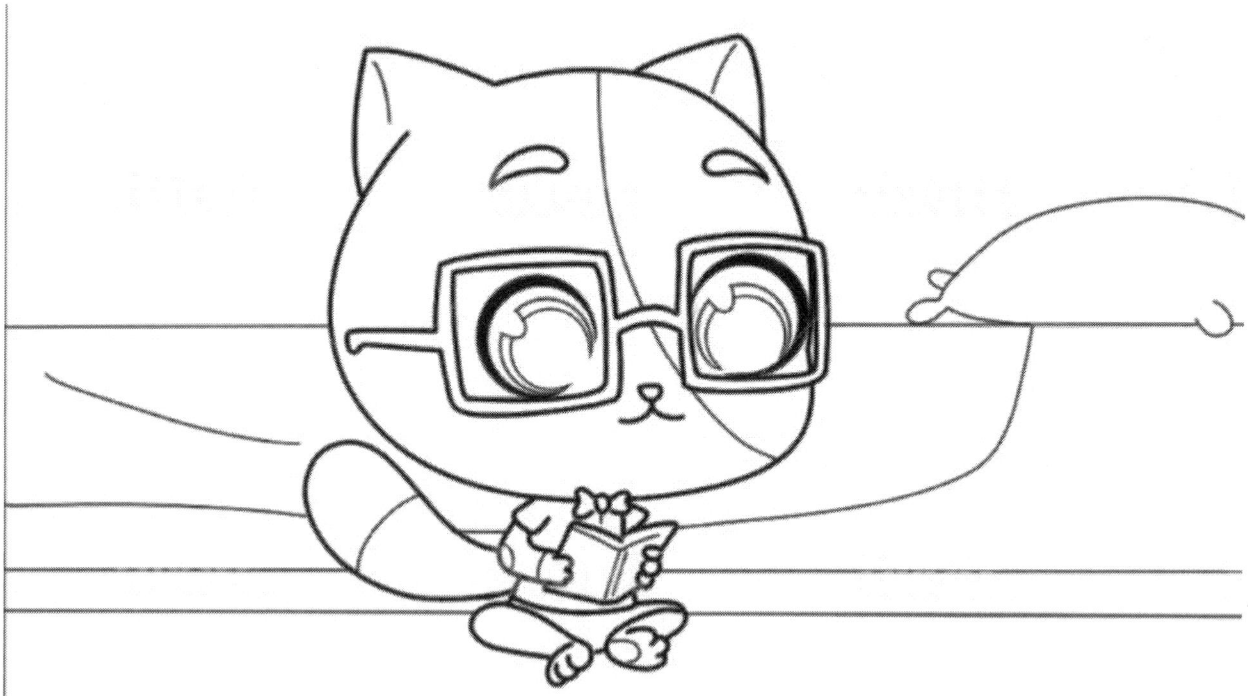

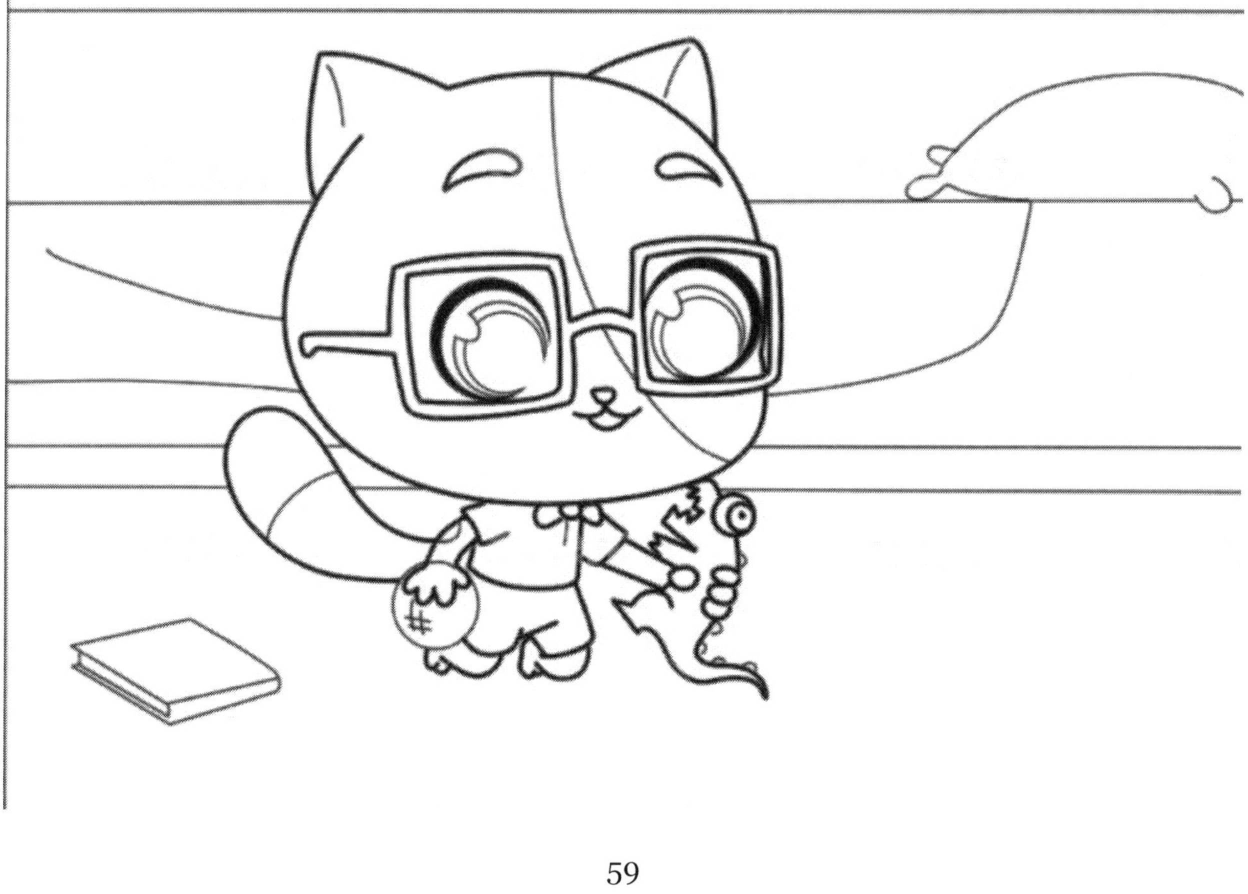

60

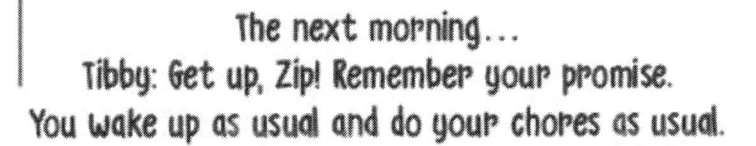

The next morning...
Tibby: Get up, Zip! Remember your promise.
You wake up as usual and do your chores as usual.

Tibby: Remember, Zip, sleep is like a treasure. We set ourselves up for a fun and energetic tomorrow when we respect our bedtime limits.

63

What Are Limits?

Limits are rules or roadblocks that help keep us safe, happy, and balanced.

Imagine a traffic light lamp. Green means go, yellow means slow down, and red means stop. These rules keep everyone safe.

Now, imagine playing your favorite game. There are also rules, no? These rules or limits help everyone play fair and have a good time. Just like in a game, limits in real life help you know what's okay and what's not—for your own good.

Limits can be about how much candy you eat, how much screen time you spend, and, yes, even when it's time to go to bed. Think of limits as your personal superhero guide! They keep you from going too far or doing things that might not benefit you.

Worksheet: The Limits Survey

Here's a quick and short survey about limits. All you need to do is answer "Yes" or "No" to each question. Again, there are no right or wrong answers, okay? Just be honest with yourself, and everything will be fine.

QUESTION	YES	NO
Do you sometimes say "Yes" when you really want to say "No?"		
Do you sometimes do things you don't want to, just because your friends want you to?		
Do you sometimes do something anyway, even if, in your heart, you know that you shouldn't?		
Is it difficult to tell other kids or adults when you don't like something they're doing or are uncomfortable around them?		
Have you ever kept playing a game even when you're tired or bored?		
Do you feel like you can't say no to grown-ups, even if you want to?		
Have you ever let someone borrow your things even though you weren't okay with it?		
Do you feel upset when someone invades your personal space without permission?		
Have you ever felt pressured to keep a secret that made you uncomfortable?		
Do you sometimes agree with your friends even when you have a different opinion?		
Have you ever continued a conversation or activity even when it made you uncomfortable?		
Have you ever felt scared to stand up for yourself?		

This survey helps you understand how you feel about your own limits. So, if you answered "Yes" to most of the questions, you probably need to set some limits—for your own good.

Setting limits doesn't mean you'll stop being kind to others. It just means you want to be kind to yourself, too.

When we set limits, we show that we value ourselves (e.g., our time, our bodies, our feelings, etc.) Being kind, friendly, considerate, and helpful to others is awesome. Still, if we forget to be kind to ourselves, we might run out of kindness to share with others. So ensure you have A LOT of kindness directed to yourself, too.

Limits are also simple ways to practice self-care, which is very important for your physical, mental, and emotional health. So, think of limits as superhero vitamins! When you take them consistently, you put yourself in the best position to be energetic and happy, enabling you to embrace all the amazing adventures life has in store!

So, now you might be thinking: What limits should I put on myself?

Many of your current limits may come from your parents or other caring adults, and they're there to keep you safe and healthy. But as you grow, you'll also learn to set your own limits based on what feels right for you. Remember, just like an artist chooses the perfect colors for their masterpiece, you also get to decide on the limits that paint your life with happiness, confidence, and success.

For now, though, here are a few things to think about. As you go through each item, think about how it can help you become your BEST SELF. That is, someone who is happy, energetic, and well-balanced.

To help you, some suggestions are provided below. However, there are no specific one-size-fits-all recommendations, so please discuss any of these topics with your parents or any trusted adult.

1. **Bedtime**. 101 studies show (okay, I may be exaggerating) that getting enough sleep is good for you. Sleep helps you grow; it helps develop your brain, ensures you have energy for tomorrow, and so much more. Your parents may have already imposed a specific bedtime for you, so the next time you don't want to follow it, think about the benefits of this limit instead.

   Suggested limit: School-aged kids should sleep around 9-12 hours per night for optimum health.[2] So, how about bedtimes of around 8:00 PM to 9:30 PM and wake-up times of around 6:0 to 7:30 AM?
   What do you think?

   _____
   _____
   _____

2. **Screen Time**. Most kids now are digital kids. Are you one of them? It's cool to have phones, tablets, and laptops, but all that screen time can be very unhealthy for your eyes.[3] So consider limiting your time in front of a screen.

   Suggested screen-time limit: 1-2 hours each day, and turn off all screens 60 minutes before bedtime.
   What do you think?

   _____
   _____
   _____

3. **Treats**. Seriously, who doesn't like candy, chocolate, cake, and all that stuff? However, eating too many sweet treats can lead to weight gain and other health problems.[4] A sweet treat now and then is perfectly fine, but think about limiting how many sugary snacks or treats you can have in a day.

   Suggested sweet treat limit: 1-2 sweet treats per day (e.g., two pieces of candy, two small pieces of chocolate, two small cookies, etc.). You can also opt for one big treat on special occasions, like a big slice of cake, but only if someone has a birthday.
   What do you think?
   _____
   _____
   _____

4. **Playtime**. Make no mistake about it: Playtime is important. But alas, there are only 24 hours a day, so if you spend too much time playing online or with your toys, you won't have enough time to do other important stuff like studying, spending time with family or friends, and others. So, think about a certain time limit you should have when it comes to playtime.

   Suggested playtime limit (offline or online): 60 minutes on school days and 2 hours on non-school days[5]
   What do you think?
   _____
   _____
   _____

5. **Personal Space.** We discussed personal space before (page 26). Now, it's time to think about it in terms of limits.

   *Example: **MY** best friend **CAN** sit beside me, **BUT** they can't lick my arm.*

Your turn:

My _____ can _____ but _____.
My _____ can _____ but _____.
My _____ can _____ but _____.
My _____ can _____ but _____.
My _____ can _____ but _____.

6. **Activities**. After-school activities or sports are great, but you might get overwhelmed if you participate in too many. Also, it might be better to excel or be really great in one thing than be so-so in 10 things, right?

   Put a checkmark next to any activity you're doing right now after school.

   ☐ Sports
   ☐ Art Classes
   ☐ Music Lessons
   ☐ Dance
   ☐ Scouting
   ☐ Language Classes
   ☐ Cooking or Baking
   ☐ Coding, Robotics, Computer-Related Stuff
   ☐ Theater or Drama
   ☐ Science Clubs
   ☐ Reading Clubs
   ☐ Community Service
   ☐ Others:

   _____
   _____

Question: Should you let go of any of these activities?
- ☐ Yes
- ☐ No

If you said **Yes**, which activities should you stop doing?

Put a cross mark *X* next to the after-school activity you want to stop.

- ☐ Sports
- ☐ Art Classes
- ☐ Music Lessons
- ☐ Dance
- ☐ Scouting
- ☐ Language Classes
- ☐ Cooking or Baking
- ☐ Coding, Robotics, Computer-Related Stuff
- ☐ Theater or Drama
- ☐ Science Clubs
- ☐ Reading Clubs
- ☐ Community Service
- ☐ Others:

_____

_____

Remember, setting limits helps you manage your time, energy, and feelings, so think about the above or anything else you might want to set limits on.

Body Safety: Recognizing When You Feel Uncomfortable

When you're inside a car, there's a super important rule: Always wear your seatbelt. This rule is for your safety.

There are speed limits when you ride your bike, and you might even need to wear a bike helmet. Why? Yep, this is to ensure your safety.

In the above examples, you protect yourself from possible physical harm, like hurting your shoulder or breaking your leg. But there are other reasons to practice safety.

Take the playground, for example. It's a land of fun and games, but it's NOT cool if someone decides to push you, yank your hair, or touch you where you don't want to be touched.

Yes, these actions can hurt your body, but they can also hurt your *feelings*. Like a puzzle with missing pieces, these not-so-nice actions by others can leave you feeling confused, sad, or even angry. So remember, protecting your body isn't just about bones and bruises; it's about guarding your heart and happiness, too.

Now, when it comes to your body, here's rule number one: **Your body, your rules**.

You're the Big Boss of your body, and you have 100% rights over it. No one should touch or invade your personal space without your permission. Your body is your treasure chest of feelings and sensations; only you can decide who can be near or touch you. So, stand tall, and remember that your body's rules are the mightiest rules of all!

Good Touch vs. Bad Touch

Let's talk about something really important: Good Touch and Bad Touch. Just like you have different feelings, there are different kinds of touches.

Good Touch is like a warm hug from Mom and Dad, a high-five, or a gentle pat on the back. These touches make you feel **happy**, **safe**, and **comfortable**. They're the kind of touches you welcome because they show care and love.

Bad Touch is when someone touches your body in a way that makes you **uncomfortable**, **scared**, or **confused**. It's like a little alarm inside you saying, "This doesn't feel right." Bad touches might include someone touching your private areas or touching you when you've said "No."

Remember, your body belongs to you, and you decide what feels okay and what doesn't. If someone gives you a bad touch, telling a trusted adult immediately is important. Trusted adults are your protectors, and they'll help you understand and handle the situation.

Worksheet: Safe People

Name at least three (3) Safe People in your universe. These are the people you trust. You can tell them anything, and they will believe you. If you ever feel scared, unsafe, or uncomfortable, you can reach out to these people immediately without any worries.

Put their pictures below or write their names and color each outline. By the way, if you have more than three Safe People, grrrrreat! Write them down, too, or get another piece of paper and draw more Safe People outlines. Awesome!

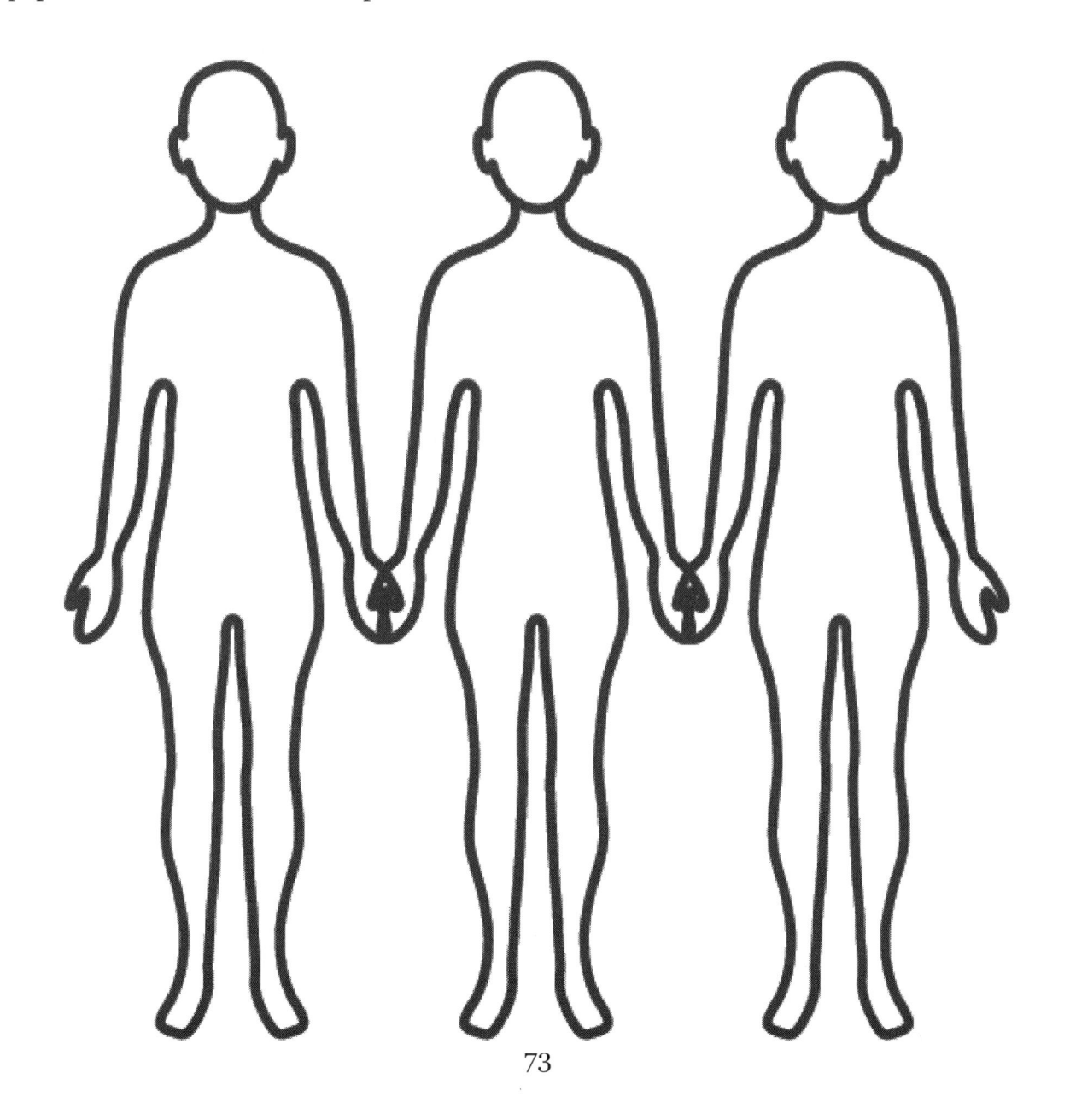

Safe Secrets vs. Unsafe Secrets

Secrets are things you know, find out on your own, or are told by someone else, and you decide (or are told by someone) not to tell other people about them. However, not all secrets are good.

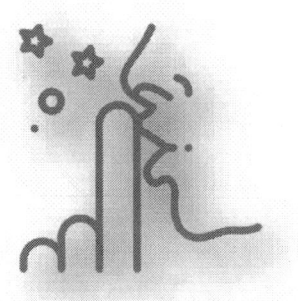

Safe Secrets are secrets that are okay to keep. They're usually about fun surprises, like planning a birthday party or keeping a special gift a secret until party time. Safe secrets make people **happy** and **excited**; they're okay to keep as long as they're **not hurting anyone**.

Unsafe Secrets are secrets that make you feel **uncomfortable**, **worried**, or **scared**. These secrets are NOT okay to keep. If someone tells you to keep a secret that involves touching you in a way that feels wrong or anything that doesn't feel right, it's really important to talk to a grown-up you trust about it. (**Tip**: Think about your Safe People list.) These grown-ups are there to make sure you're safe and happy, and they can help you decide what to do with the secret.

Remember, your feelings matter, and you should never keep a secret that doesn't feel right.

Listening to Your Gut

Listening to your gut is like having a little detective inside you that helps you know what's right and wrong. It's that little voice in your tummy that tells you when something feels good or when something doesn't feel quite right.

For example, if you're about to try something new and your tummy feels excited, that's your gut saying, "Oooh, this is scary, but this could be fun too!" On the other hand, if someone asks you to do something and it makes your tummy feel funny in a bad way, that's your gut telling you to be careful. So, always pay attention to that feeling in your belly. That little detective in there is making sure you make good choices and stay safe and happy.

Worksheet: Warning Feelings

Write down words to describe what happens to your body when you feel uncomfortable.

Examples: eyes -> you feel like crying; tummy -> you feel like there are butterflies in there, etc.

The next time you feel anything like what you wrote above, your gut might be trying to tell you something isn't right or safe. When this happens, talk to one of your Safe People.

Saying "No"

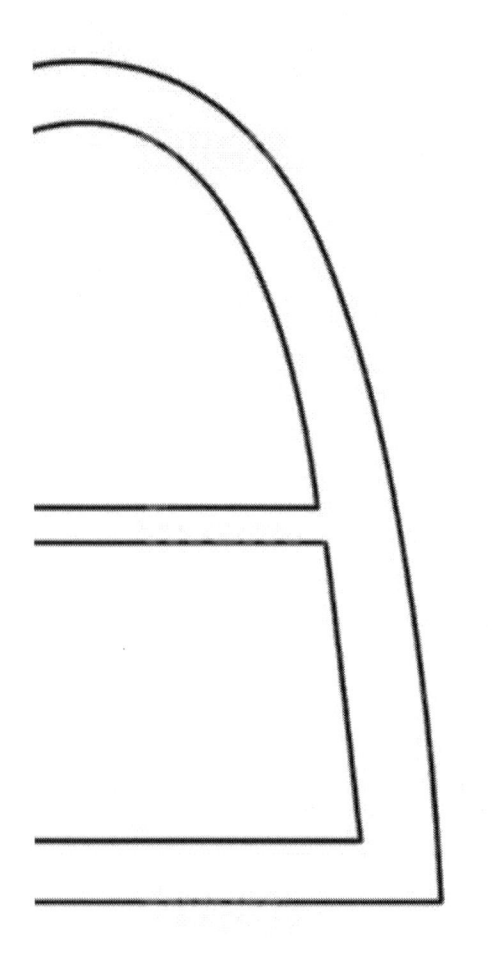

Tibby: Zip, no! That's my toy.
Zip: Let's play with it now.
Tibby: No!

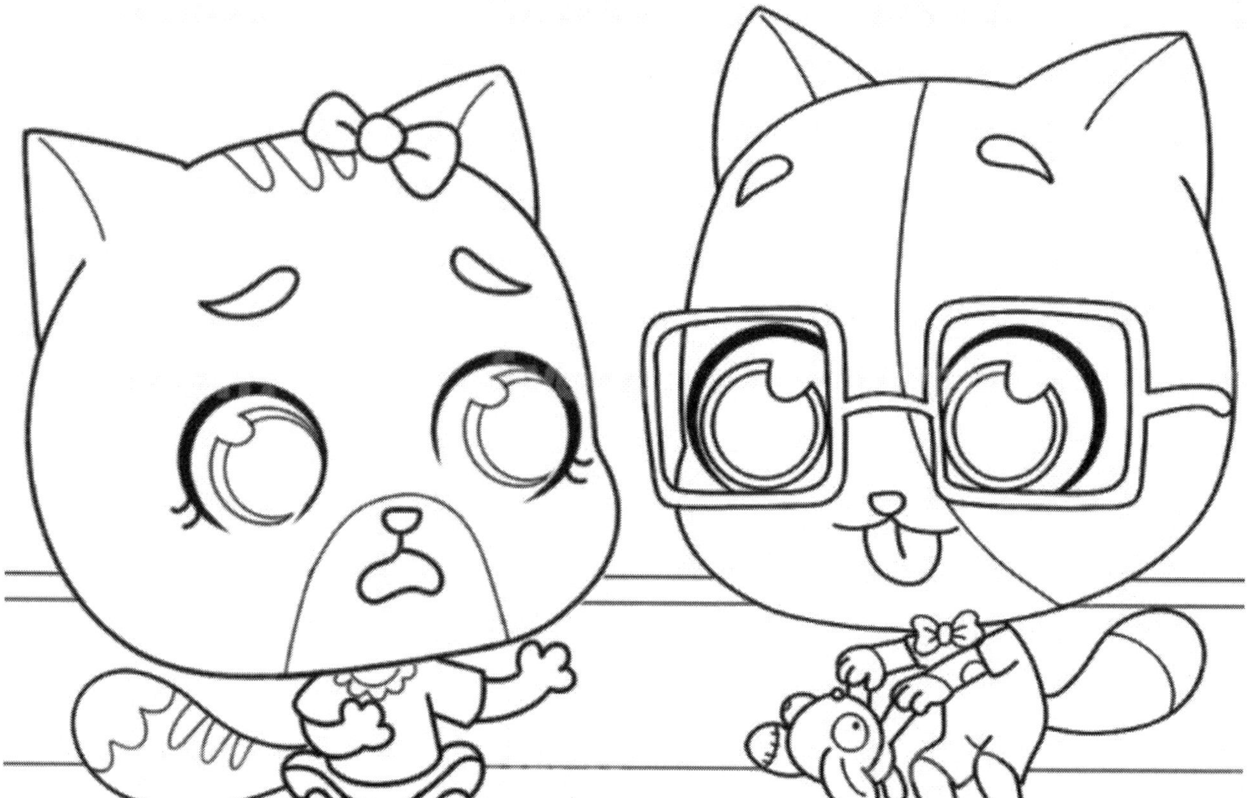

80

Tibby: Zip, that toy is a special gift from Grammy.
So I want to be extra careful with it. It doesn't mean
I'll never ever want to play with it with you.
Zip: Okay.
Tibby: And you don't need to be sad when I say "No," Zip.
I'm not mad at you, but you must respect it
when I say "No."
Zip: I understand. Sorry, Tibby.

What Does Saying "No" Mean?

Saying "No" is a way of telling someone that you don't want to do something or are uncomfortable with a situation.

Imagine you have a magic shield, like the ones knights use in stories. This shield helps protect your feelings, your space, and your things. When you say "No," it's like raising your shield to protect yourself.

Saying "No" doesn't mean you're being rude or unkind. It's a way of caring for yourself and respecting your feelings. Just like you'd use your magic shield to defend yourself from dragons or monsters, saying "No" helps defend your feelings and boundaries. It's a powerful way to show that you're in control of your choices and listen to what feels right.

So, if someone says something, does something, or asks you to do something that makes you uncomfortable, remember that saying "No" is your superhero power. It's a shield that helps you stay true to your needs and wants.

When Should You Say "No?"

Saying "No" is an important superpower, but when should you use this amazing gift? Here are some situations when saying "No" is important:

1. **When you feel uncomfortable**. If something doesn't feel right in your tummy or makes you worried, saying "No" can help you avoid unsafe or unenjoyable things.

2. **When your boundaries are crossed.** If someone tries to touch you or come too close when you don't want them to, it's okay to say "No." Your body, your rules!

3. **When you need space.** If you're feeling overwhelmed or need some time alone, saying "No" lets others know you need your personal space.

4. **When you have too much to do.** If your schedule is busy or you're tired, saying "No" to extra things can help you avoid feeling overwhelmed.

5. **When something doesn't feel right.** Trust your feelings. If something doesn't seem okay, saying "No" is your way of staying safe and true to yourself.

6. **When you want to prioritize yourself.** You don't always have to have a BIG reason to say "No." For example, if you already have other plans or are not in the mood for what others want to do, it's still okay to say "No."

Remember, saying "No" is a way to keep yourself safe, happy, and comfortable. It's your choice, and using it when necessary is always okay.

How to Say "No"

We've had some great conversations about your personal space (your private bubble), your limits (your personal do's and don'ts), and your boundaries (the things you're comfortable with and those you're not). We also discussed why saying " No " is important if people start pushing or crossing your boundaries. But if saying "No" is so important—why is it sometimes so hard to say?!

Sometimes, saying "No" can be tricky because you want to make your family, friends, or others happy. You might worry that if you say "No," people will be disappointed, sad, or even mad at you. I know being liked is important to you, so you might feel like saying "No" could change how others feel about you. Sometimes, you may feel scared to say "No" because you're unsure about something.

Also, when you care about someone's feelings, you might not want to hurt them by saying "No." For example, you might think that if you say "No" to a friend, they might feel sad or left out. This can make you feel like you must say "Yes" even when you don't want to.

Another reason saying "No" can be tough is when you might not want to seem "different." If everyone else is doing the same thing, you might feel pressure to join in, even if you don't feel comfortable doing it.

It's okay sometimes to have doubts and confusion about these things—it's completely normal! Learning to say "No" takes practice, and as you get older, you'll become more confident in making choices that feel right for you. Just remember that if something bothers you or doesn't feel right, it's better to be safe than sorry and say "No"—even if you're unsure.

So, I guess the next big question is this: HOW do you say "No?"

The best way to say "No" is to be kind but confident. You want others to understand your feelings but don't want to look bossy or upset. Keep the following in mind, okay?

1. **Use a kind tone.** When saying "No," use a gentle and friendly voice.
2. **Look kindly into the other person's eyes.** If you're comfortable, look at the person in the eyes. It shows you're being honest and sincere.
3. **Be polite.** Start with a polite word, like "Thanks," "Thank you," or "I appreciate it," before saying "No." For example, "Thanks for wanting me with you guys, but **no**, I don't want to skip school today."
4. **To explain or not to explain**. Although saying "No" should be enough, sometimes it helps keep the situation cool if you say something about why you're saying no. Keep it simple, and say something like "I can't today" or "Oh, I'm just not in the mood." You can even make it funny, "Oh, I can't go with you guys, bad tummy ache. Lots and lots of gas..."
5. **Suggest another idea.** If you can, offer another solution. For example, say, "I can't play now, but maybe we can play this weekend?"
6. **Stay confident.** Believe in your decision to say no. If you're confident, others are more likely to understand and accept your choice. You can practice saying no in front of a mirror if you're shy. Stand up tall, straighten your shoulders, look yourself in the eye, and say "No" with confidence.
7. **Use "I" Statements.** Use phrases that start with "I" to express *your* feelings, like "I would rather not," "I'm not comfortable," or "I don't want to."
8. **Stick to your decision.** If someone tries to change your mind, be polite, but don't change your mind. You can say, "Thank you, but I'm still going to say 'No'."

Remember, saying "No" is about caring for yourself and communicating your boundaries. It's an important skill that helps you build healthy relationships and make the right choices.

Worksheet: Saying No Thinking Cards

It's practice time! Following are a few thinking cards to help you consider different situations and make thoughtful choices about when to say "Yes," when to say "No," and how to express your choices.

I'm not going to give any examples, okay? I want you to put your thinking caps on and practice what you want to say and do in these situations.

The Sharing Dilemma

Your friend wants to borrow your favorite book/toy/sweater, etc., for a whole week!

Do you feel comfortable lending your fav item? Should you say "Yes" or "No?"

Even if you say "Yes," you want to ensure your friend returns the item after a week. How do you communicate this?

The Not-So-Funny Joke

Classmate A is daring you to steal Classmate B's lunch and throw it as a "joke." But you know in your heart that it's a very mean thing to do.

What should you do?
What should you say?

The Personal Space Challenge

An adult keeps standing too close to you in the library.

Should you let them invade your personal space, or should you say "No" and ask your space to be respected?

The Extra Activity Invite

Your friend invites you to an after-school club, but you're already in another one you like.

Should you join the new club and leave the club you're in right now, or say "No" and continue what you're already doing?

The Sleepover Twist

Woohoo! You're invited to a sleepover; it's so exciting! But they want to watch a scary movie. You don't like this because horror movies give you nightmares.

Should you watch the movie anyway, or should you say "No" and suggest to watch something else?

The Personal Information Ask

Someone you just met asks for your phone number.

Is sharing your phone number with this stranger/new acquaintance okay, or should you say "No" and protect your privacy?

Accepting "No" from Others

EVERYONE has their own personal space, limits, and boundaries. This means that other people can say "No" too, and it's very important you understand and accept this.

So, when a family member, friend, or classmate says "No" to you, here's how to handle it:

1. **Respect their "No."** Just like you have the right to say "No," so do others. If someone says "No" to playing a game or sharing something, respect it. If you do that, there's a great chance they will also respect you when you say "No."

2. **Don't push.** If someone says "No," don't keep asking or trying to change their mind. It's their choice, and nagging them might make them uncomfortable.

3. **Ask nicely.** If you're curious why someone said "No," you can ask politely. For example, you can say, "Oh, okay. Do you mind telling me why?" But if the other person doesn't want to explain, respect that, too.

4. **Stay kind**. Remember that saying "No" is about taking care of yourself, so if someone says "No" to you, they're prioritizing themselves in that situation or moment.

5. **Don't take it personally.** When someone says "No," it doesn't mean they don't like you. For example, if you want to meet up and have a playdate and your friend doesn't want to and says "No," that doesn't mean they never want to play with you again. Just not now or today.

   Here's another example: if your parents say "No" to something you want, like eating extra candy or going somewhere alone with other kids, this doesn't mean they're trying to punish you. They might say "No" to keep you safe and healthy.

6. **Suggest alternatives.** Suppose you suggested that your best friend come over so that you can do your schoolwork together, and they said no. Suggest an alternative like, "What about tomorrow?" or "What if I go to your place?"

Remember, just like you want others to understand and respect your "No," it's important to do the same for them. Everyone has their own feelings and boundaries, and it's part of being a good person to honor and accept those choices.

Exploring Your Boundary Universe!

Zip: Wow, there are so many stars!
The world is so big, right, Tibby?

Tibby: You know, Zip, you're right. The world is really big and beautiful. But you know what? I think our world is like a big universe of boundaries. Just like every star in the night sky has its unique place, so do different types of boundaries.

Zip: Like what?

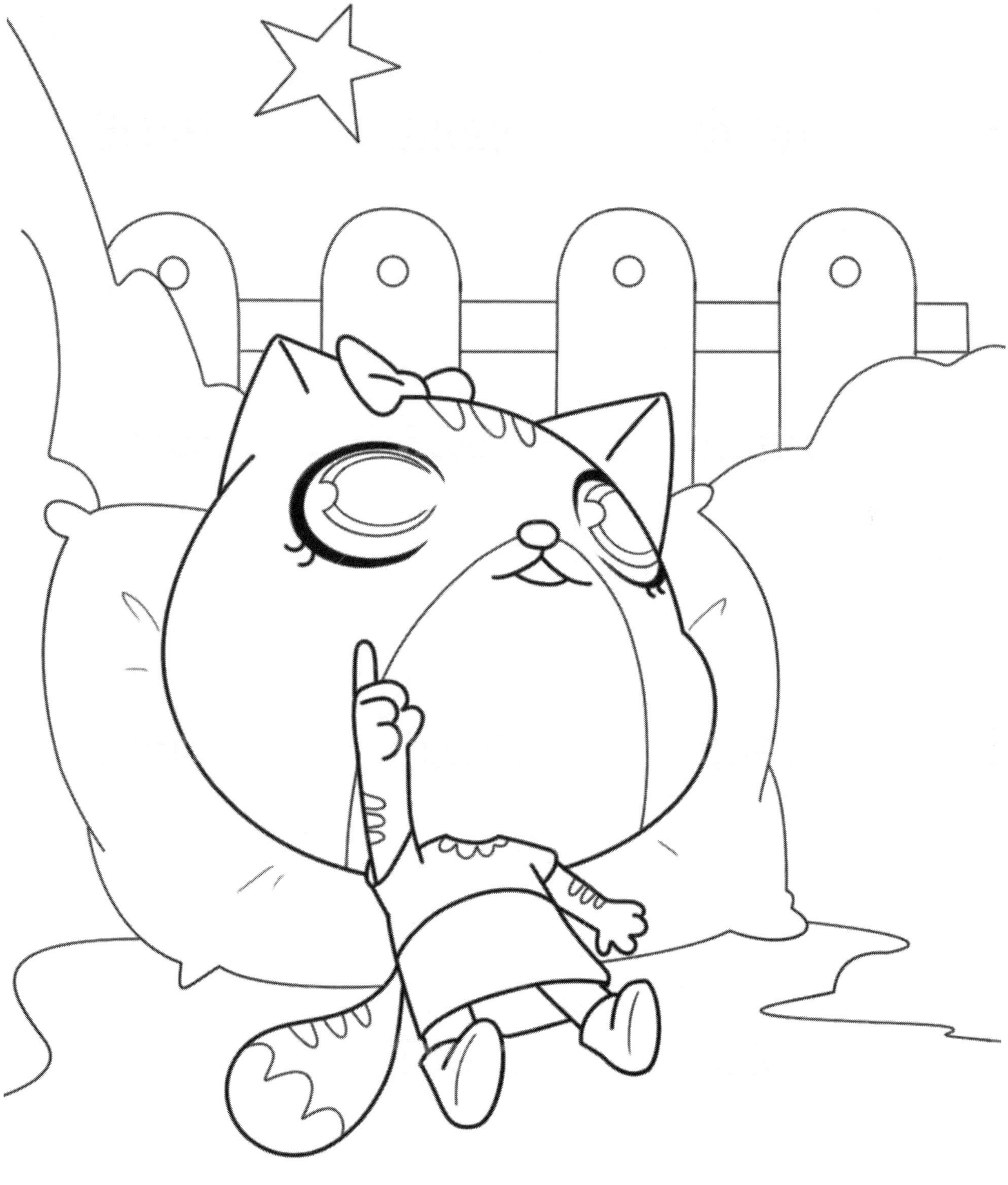

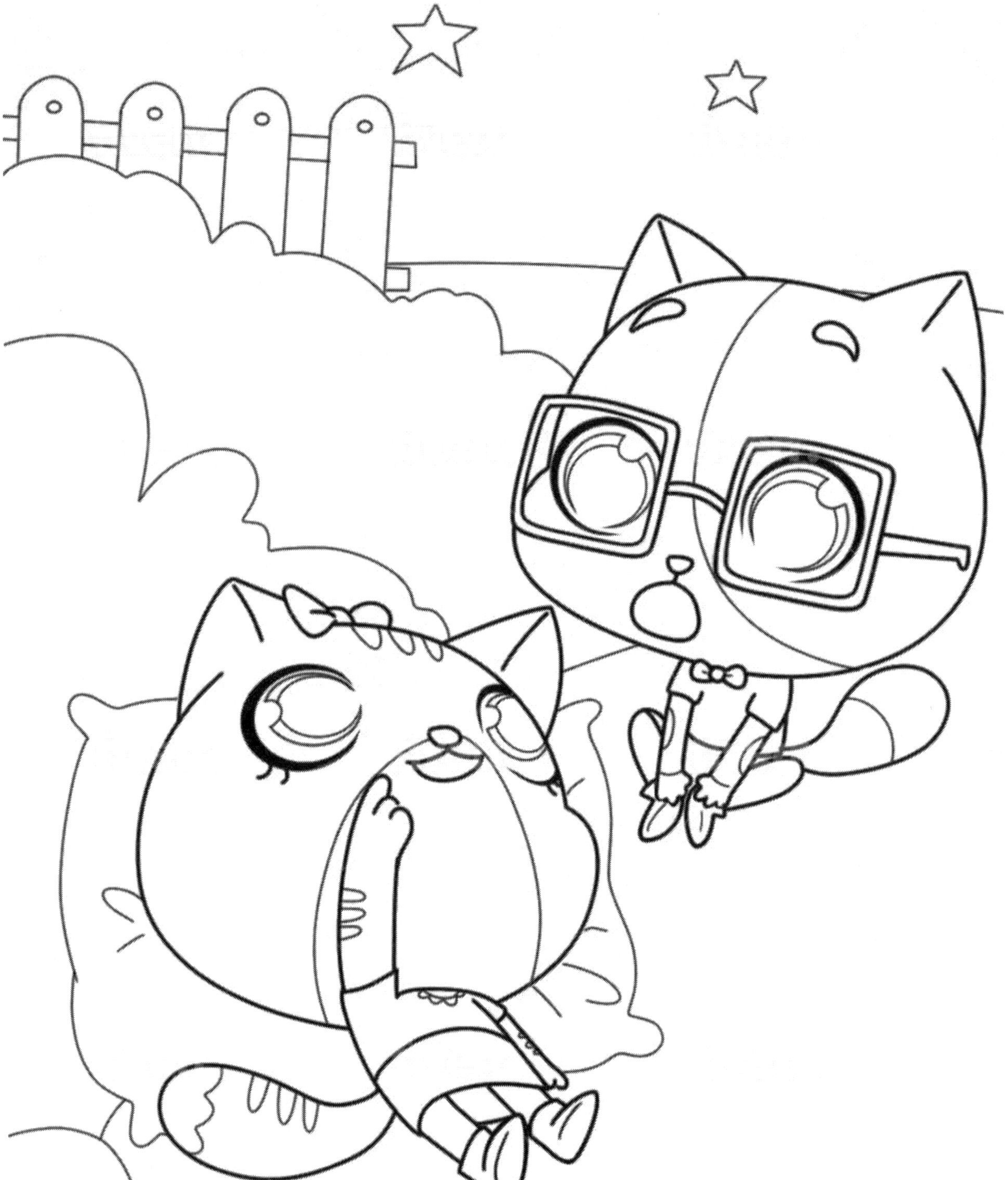

Tibby: Well, see that big star over there? Imagine that as our home.
So that star has "family boundaries" in it.
They help us understand what's okay to share within our family
and what might be better to keep private.
It's like having little secrets that strengthen our family bond.

Zip: Wow!

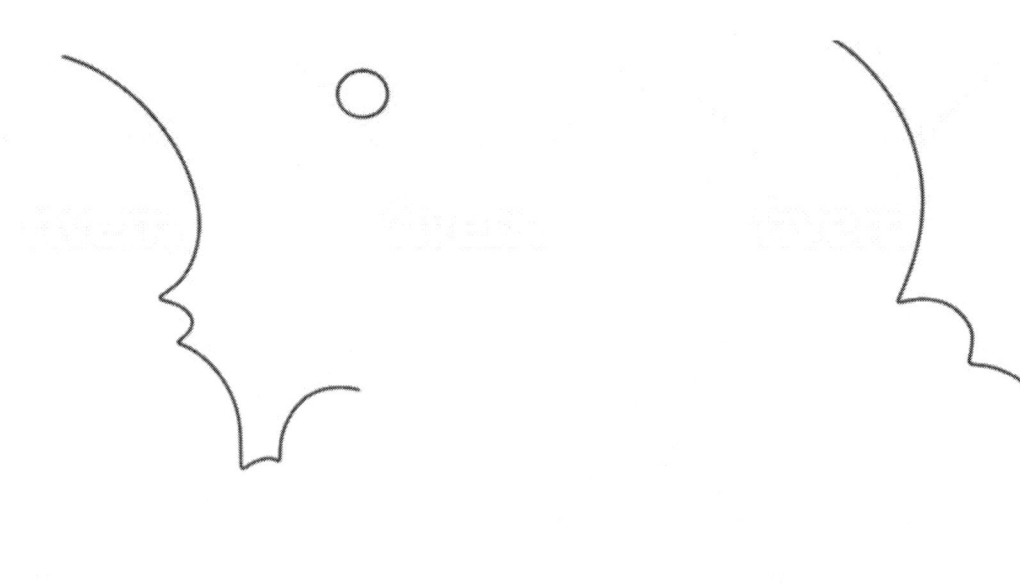

Tibby: See that beautiful blinking star next to our "Home" star? Imagine that as yourself. So, that magical star represents our emotional boundaries.

Zip: Emotional boundaries?

Tibby: Yes, Zip. Those are the rules that help us understand our own feelings and the feelings of others.

97

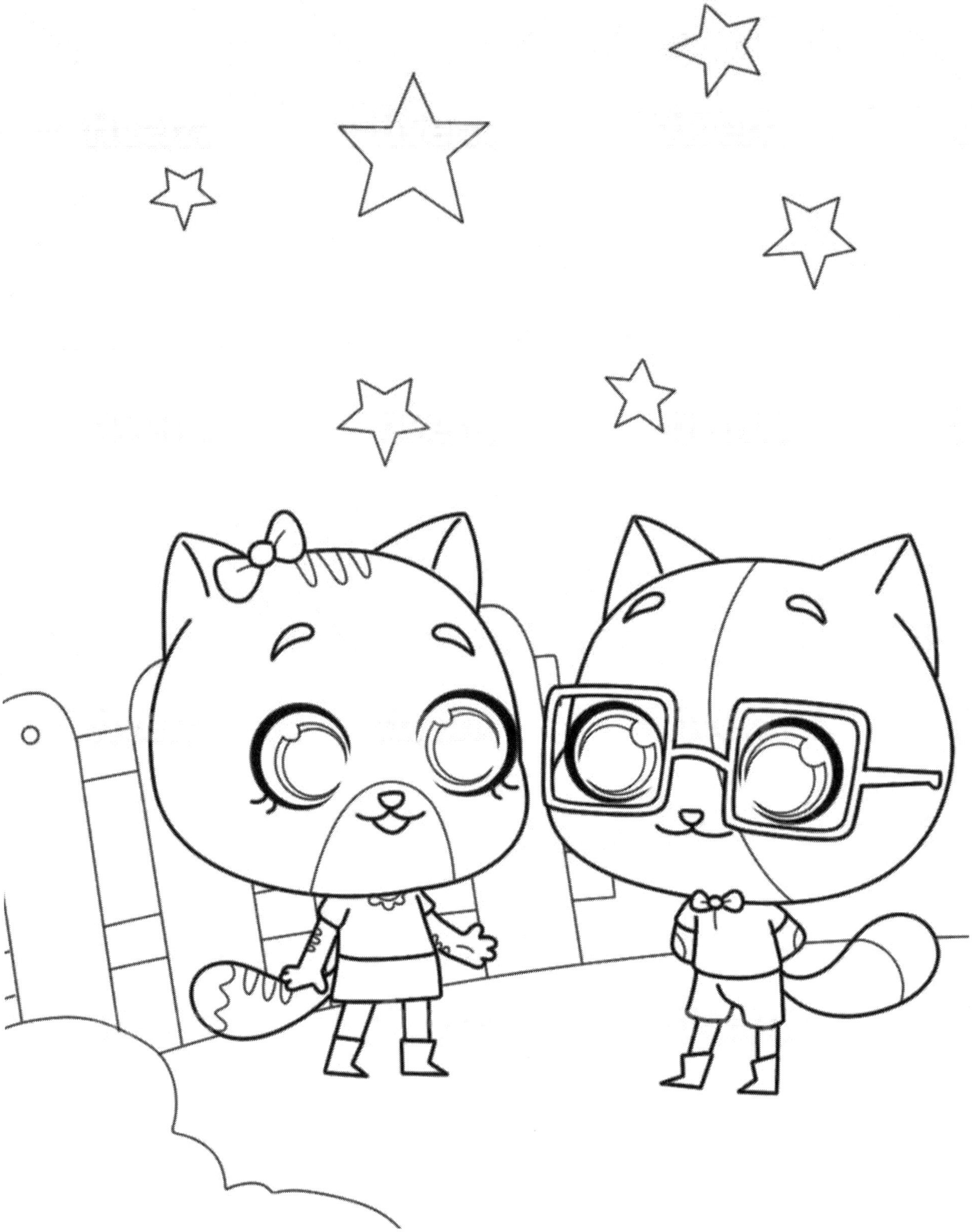

Tibby: Look up, Zip. There are many stars in the sky, right?

Zip: Uh-huh.

Tibby: So that means there are many other types of boundaries, too!

Zip: [eyes huge] There are?!

Tibby: Oh, sure! Come on, grab that telescope, and we'll go explore them!

Worksheet: Mindfulness Rainbow Breathing

Hey, kids! Before you go exploring the different types of boundaries with Tibby and Zip, let's do a calming exercise first.

This will help you relax and focus, so you're super ready to explore different boundaries in the next pages.

Ready? Let's get started!

1. **Sit in a comfortable position**, either on the floor or in a chair, whatever you like! Ensure your back is straight and your hands are resting gently on your lap.

2. **If you feel like it, close your eyes.** If not, you can softly gaze at a spot on the floor in front of you.

3. Now, **take a deep breath in through your nose**. Feel your belly rise as you fill your lungs with air.

4. Next, **exhale slowly through your mouth**. Imagine that you're blowing away any stress or worries.

5. Here comes the exciting part: **Imagine a beautiful rainbow** in front of you, its colors shining brightly!

6. **Breathe in**, and as you do, **imagine breathing in the color red**. Feel the warmth of the color red filling your body.

7. **Exhale slowly**, and as you do, let go of any tension or stress. **Imagine the color red slowly leaving your body** as you breathe out.

8. Repeat slowly breathing in and breathing out while imagining the other colors of the rainbow.
    - **Orange**. Breathe in orange, feeling its **energy and brightness**.
    - **Yellow**. Breathe in yellow, feeling its **warmth and joy**.
    - **Green**. Breathe in green, feeling its **calmness and balance**.
    - **Blue**. Breathe in blue, feeling its **serenity and peace**.
    - **Indigo**. Breathe in indigo, feeling its **clarity and focus**.
    - **Violet**. Breathe in violet, feeling its **relaxation and stillness**.

9. Finally, imagine yourself surrounded by a beautiful rainbow of colors. Feel their positive vibes, embracing you like a warm, protective, loving hug.

10. When you're ready, take one last deep breath through your nose and exhale slowly through your mouth.

11. If your eyes were closed, gently open them. Take a moment to notice how you feel – calm, relaxed, and centered.

Use this exercise whenever you need a moment of calmness and relaxation.

Family and Home Boundaries

Welcome to the fascinating world of Family and Home Boundaries! In this section, you'll learn how to navigate the shared spaces, feelings, and secrets that strengthen a family. Explore the joys and challenges of living under the same roof and how understanding and respecting each other's boundaries can create harmony in your Home universe.

Sharing and Respecting Spaces and Belongings

Imagine your home as a treasure map; every room is a unique zone on that map. Now, some zones are for absolute sharing.

For example, the living room is where the whole family gets together to watch movies or play games. It's a shared zone for laughter and bonding. Another shared zone is the kitchen. It's where the magic of cooking and eating as a family happens.
Your bedroom, however, is a unique zone on your home map. It's your own little kingdom. It's where your personal treasures are, like your toys, books, and secrets. This means that other people should respect this space.

For example, you can tell your parents or siblings that they should always knock first before entering your room. You can also tell them not to take anything from your room, even if it's just to borrow it, without first asking for your permission.

Remember that your parents and siblings also have their own bedrooms and sanctuaries, so you should also respect *their* boundaries. For example, suppose you like to play loud video games, but your sibling is preparing hard for an exam. In this situation, their boundary might be about loud noises. So, don't be noisy so they can concentrate on their school stuff.

Sharing and respecting each other's personal spaces and boundaries are important to keep peace and harmony in a family. When everyone respects these boundaries, it means fewer arguments and more happiness for everyone at home!

Worksheet: My Bedroom Boundaries

Your bedroom is your special zone in the Home universe. It's a place where you can be yourself and feel cozy. But have you ever thought about what's okay and what's not when it comes to your bedroom and all your stuff? Let's go do some bedroom boundary exploration!

1. **My Treasures**: Draw, write, or cut and paste pictures of your favorite things in your bedroom. These could be toys, books, or anything special to you.

2. **My Personal Space**: Draw, write, or cut and paste pictures of your favorite spot in your bedroom. It could be your bed, a comfy chair, or a corner where you like to read or play.

3. **My Bedroom Self-Boundary Rules**: Think about some rules YOU should follow to help keep your bedroom cozy, organized, and fun.

   Examples:
   I'll put my dirty clothes in the hamper mom put in the bathroom.
   I'll fix my bed before I go to school.
   Rule #1. _____
   Rule #2. _____
   Rule #3. _____
   Rule #4. _____
   Rule #5. _____

4. **Rules for Other People**: Think about your boundaries (i.e., what you like and don't like) so that others understand and follow them.

   Example: *I don't like it when mom goes in without knocking, especially when I have friends over.*
   Rule #1. _____
   Rule #2. _____
   Rule #3. _____
   Rule #4. _____
   Rule #5. _____

5. **Sharing Time**: When family members or friends enter your room, think about what you're happy to share with them and what you want to keep for yourself. Letting them know what's okay and what's not is important.

I'm okay sharing my:

Examples: *books, board games, toys, art supplies*

- _____
- _____
- _____
- _____
- _____

I'm not okay sharing my:

Examples: *clothes, journal, mobile phone, bed*

- _____
- _____
- _____
- _____
- _____

6. **Special Time**: Your bedroom is where you sleep and relax. Draw, write, or cut and paste pictures about a special time you like to have in your bedroom, like reading a bedtime story, listening to music, or playing quietly.

7. **My Feelings**: How do you feel when your bedroom is just how you like it? Draw, write, or cut and paste pictures about how you feel.

Balancing Time with Family and Friends

Imagine your life is a bit like being a superhero with two amazing worlds to explore—the Family World and the Friends World.

Family World: This is your secret base, your headquarters. Your family loves you no matter what and always supports you. They know everything about you, from your favorite ice cream flavor to your funniest jokes. Just like superheroes have their special gear, your family is where you get your unique qualities, traditions, and stories. You have shared adventures and are all part of the same super team.

Friends World: This is like an exciting adventure land filled with friends who are just as awesome as you are! You can meet them at school, the park, or even your neighborhood. Friends have different stories, superpowers, and games to share. Together, you can explore new places, try new things, and have many fun adventures.

The cool thing is you can be a superhero in both worlds! In your Family World, you learn about values, traditions, and how to be a good person. You practice teamwork, sharing, and making new memories in your Friends World.

Remember, even though these worlds might seem different, they're both important parts of your superhero journey. You learn from each world and grow stronger and wiser as you go. That's why it's important to BALANCE your time in both these worlds. How?

Well, imagine having a magical calendar that can stretch to fit all your plans. Family events are on one side; on the other, there are plans with friends. Sounds cool? Well, let's go check out that calendar, then.

Worksheet: My Family and Friends Calendar

Let's practice finding the perfect balance between spending time with family and friends by imagining your days like a calendar.

1. In the 7-day calendar below, label some days as "Family Time" and others as "Friends Time."

	Morning	**Afternoon**	**Evening**
SUN	*Example:* *Family Time* Family pancake breakfasts.	*Example:* *Friends Time* Go to the mall together.	*Example:* *Family Time* Sunday dinner at Grandma.
SUN			
MON			
TUE			
WED			

	Morning	**Afternoon**	**Evening**
THU			
FRI			
SAT			

2. **Family Time.** Think of a fun family event you enjoy, like a game night or movie night. Describe below what you like about it.

   Family Time:

   Example: I love movie nights (Saturday) because we're all together. Mom makes LOTS of popcorn. Dad is home and not working, and I can choose what to watch!

   _____
   _____
   _____
   _____

3. **Friend Time.** What's your favorite thing to do with your friends? Describe below what you like about it.

   Friend Time:

   Example: My friends and I love cookies, so I like it when we have a baking afternoon at my friend Lucy's house.

_____
_____
_____
_____

4. **Flexibility**. Oops, change of plans! Sometimes, things don't go according to plans, and that's okay; that's life. You might get sad or disappointed, but the important thing is to learn to cope well. In the space below, think about a time when plans might change and what you might do about it.

Family Adjustment Situation:

Example: Mom has an important work deadline, so Saturday movie night is canceled. ☹ That's okay; I know work is also super important. I'll just ask Dad to make lots of popcorn anyway. ☺

_____
_____
_____

Friends Adjustment Situation:

Example: Lucy isn't feeling well, so the baking afternoon is canceled—bummer ☹ I think I'll just have some quiet reading time at home.

_____
_____
_____

Important: The secret to finding the perfect balance between family and friends is not about the number of minutes you spend with them but ensuring you're fully present wherever you are. When you're with your family, be with them with all your heart. And when you're with your friends, be with them with all your excitement.

Friends and Social Boundaries

As we mentioned in the previous section, your Friends World is important. And one of the ways to ensure that friendships are nothing but positive and happy experiences is to have boundaries.

What's equally fascinating about the Friends World is that, much like the countless stars in the sky, friends come in various shapes, sizes, and distances from your heart. You could be talking to someone new who could become a good friend at any given time. Or you might be chatting with your bestie, whom you've known for years!

Meeting and Making New Friends

Meeting new friends is like discovering new planets in your galaxy. But since you don't know each other really well yet, it's important to be aware of certain boundaries you might want with these people. For example, you might not want them standing too close to you or giving you tight hugs, even if they mean well.

Is there anything else you don't like people you just met doing? Write them down here!

_____
_____
_____
_____
_____

Your Closest, Bestest Friends!

Just because you really like your closest friends doesn't mean that EVERYTHING is allowed. Boundaries with besties are also super important. For example, if you share a secret with your bestie, like your school crush, you expect them NOT to tell others about it, right? So that's a best friend boundary—no spilling of each other's secrets!

Is there anything else that you don't like your closest friends to do? Write them down here!

_____

_____

_____

_____

Peer Pressure

"Peer pressure" is when your friends or people your age try to convince you to do something, even if you're not sure it's a good idea. It's like when they want you to play a game you don't like or eat or drink something you don't want to. It's important to make choices that feel right for you, even if your friends are doing something else.

Peer pressure can be tough to handle because everyone wants to "belong" and be liked by their friends. When your friends or classmates want you to do something, it can make you feel worried that if you say "no," they might not like you as much. Of course, it's natural to want to be part of a group and feel accepted. But sometimes, what they want you to do may not be best for you.

It can be hard to make the right decision, especially when you're worried about what your friends will think. That's why it's important to be strong and make choices that you believe are right, even if it's not what everyone else is doing. Also, remember that your TRUE FRIENDS will respect your choices, and it's always okay to say "no" when something doesn't feel right to you.

Worksheet: Peer Pressure at School

Peer pressure is when your friends or classmates try to convince you to do something, even if you're uncomfortable. Let's explore how to handle peer pressure at school.

1. List of Activities

Write down activities or situations where you might face peer pressure at school.

Examples: *during lunchtime, while playing a game, while doing schoolwork with classmates, etc.*

- _____
- _____
- _____
- _____
- _____

2. Saying "No" Practice

Write a polite way to say "No" for each situation you listed above.

Example: *Thanks for the invite, guys, but no. I don't want to skip school after lunch.*

- _____
- _____
- _____
- _____
- _____

3. Trusted Adult

Who is a trusted adult you can talk to if you ever feel uneasy due to peer pressure? Write down their name and how you can reach them. **Tip**: You can put the name of one of your Safe People (page 73) here.

Name: _____

Contact: _____

4. True Friends

Think about your friends at school. True friends respect your feelings and choices. Write the names of friends you can count on to support you in making good decisions.

- _____
- _____
- _____
- _____
- _____

5. Good Choices

Describe a situation where you made a good or the right choice, even when others pressured you to do something else. How did it make you feel?

Example:

Situation: *Some of my classmates planned to cheat on an upcoming exam and wanted me to be part of it. It was hard, but I said "No."*

How I felt: *I really felt the pressure to just do it and be part of the group. But cheating is not cool, and I wanted a good grade because I studied well, not because I cheated.*

Situation:
_____
_____
_____
_____
_____

How I felt:

_____
_____
_____
_____
_____
_____

Remember, saying " No " is okay if something doesn't feel right. You control your choices, and true friends will respect your decisions. Stay strong!

Feelings Boundaries

Feelings Boundaries are like the rules that help you understand your emotions, which are the feelings we have inside. Just like many colors in a crayon box, there are many feelings we can have.

For example:

Happy: This is when you feel really good and smile a lot. It's like a sunny day at the park.
Sad: When you're sad, you might feel like crying. It's okay to be sad sometimes, just like when it rains.
Angry: This is when you feel mad or upset. It's like when you can't find your favorite toy.
Excited: When something fun is about to happen, you might feel excited. It's like getting a surprise gift.
Scared: Feeling scared is when something makes you feel afraid. It's like seeing a big, mean-looking dog for the first time.

Feelings are like the colors of your heart. Sometimes, feeling all of them is okay, just like using all the colors in your crayon box when drawing a picture. Understanding your feelings and learning how to express them in a way that doesn't hurt you or others is important. That's what "feelings boundaries" are all about!

Important: Feelings are never wrong, so you should never hide, ignore, or be ashamed of them. Think of it this way: Feelings are like messengers telling you how you're experiencing the world. Just like you listen to a friend when they talk to you, it's also a good idea to listen to your emotions. They can help you understand what's happening inside you.

So, now that you know your emotions are important, here are some boundaries to consider about feelings.

Sharing Feelings: It's okay to share your feelings with someone you trust, like a parent or a friend. But keeping some feelings private is also okay if you're uncomfortable talking about them or not ready to share them yet. Remember, these are *your* feelings; you're the boss on whether you want to share them.

Respecting Others' Feelings: Just like you want others to respect your feelings, you should respect their feelings too. For example, suppose a friend is really sad about a low grade they got on an exam and feels like crying. However, you don't feel the same even though you're score was also not amazing. Understand and respect their sadness in this situation, even if you don't share it.

Taking Breaks from Strong Feelings: If you're feeling overwhelmed or really upset, it's okay to take a break from your emotions. It's okay to say, "I can't handle this right now. I need some time to calm down." Next, find a quiet place to sit and think about why you feel that way.

Asking for Help: If you're feeling really sad, scared, or confused, it's okay to ask for help from a grown-up you trust. They can help you understand and manage your emotions.

Positive Self-Talk: Sometimes, the focus of unpleasant emotions (e.g., anger, disappointment, embarrassment, etc.) is yourself. This can happen when you make a mistake, get a low grade, etc. But don't be too hard on yourself because no one is perfect. Use kind words when you talk to yourself, especially when you make mistakes.

Worksheet: Emotions Crossword

Based on the clues provided, fill in the crossword with the correct emotions or feelings.

118

Across

1 - This emotion happens when you lose something you love.

4 - You feel this when something pleasantly unexpected happens.

6 - You feel this when you've achieved something you worked hard for.

8 - You feel this when you've done something wrong.

Down

2 - The feeling of being very, very excited.

3 - Feeling content and satisfied.

4 - The opposite of happy.

5 - When something makes you laugh a lot, you feel ____ in your heart.

7 - Feeling scared or frightened.

Body Boundaries

Body Boundaries are rules that help you understand and protect your body. Your body belongs to you, and it is important to know how to keep it safe and comfortable.

Your body is inside your personal space (that invisible bubble around you). We also discussed what's okay and what's not with [Good Touch vs. Bad Touch](#) (page 71), but here are more examples of body boundaries.

No Touching Without Permission!
Nobody should touch your body without your permission, except for grown-ups who help care for you, like parents or doctors. If someone tries to touch you when you don't want them to, it's okay to say "No" and tell a trusted adult.

Private Parts Stay Private
Some parts of your body are private, like your chest and private area. It's important to keep these parts covered and not show them to anyone, except for trusted grown-ups, when they need to help you with things like bathing or going to the doctor.

Use the Right Words
It's smart to know the proper names for your body parts, like "penis," "vagina," or "breasts." This helps you talk to somebody about your body if needed.

Your Body, Your Choice
You have the right to decide what you do with your body. If you don't want to hug or kiss someone, that's okay.

If someone makes you feel uncomfortable about your body boundaries or touches you in a way that doesn't feel right, tell a trusted adult immediately. They will help keep you safe.

Worksheet: Touching

Do you know the swimsuit rule? It means that whatever your swimsuit covers is a NO-TOUCH zone. But what about other parts of your body?

For example, if it's bedtime, then mom and dad can lean in for a goodnight kiss on your cheek, right? So, I want you to grab a pencil or crayon, color your cheek, and say, "Mom and Dad, okay to kiss." This means that if *someone else* kisses you or tries to kiss you on your cheek and you don't like it, you must go to one of your Safe People (page 73) and tell them. Got it? Cool! So, go ahead and have a good think and go doodle or color away on the picture below about who can touch your body and where.

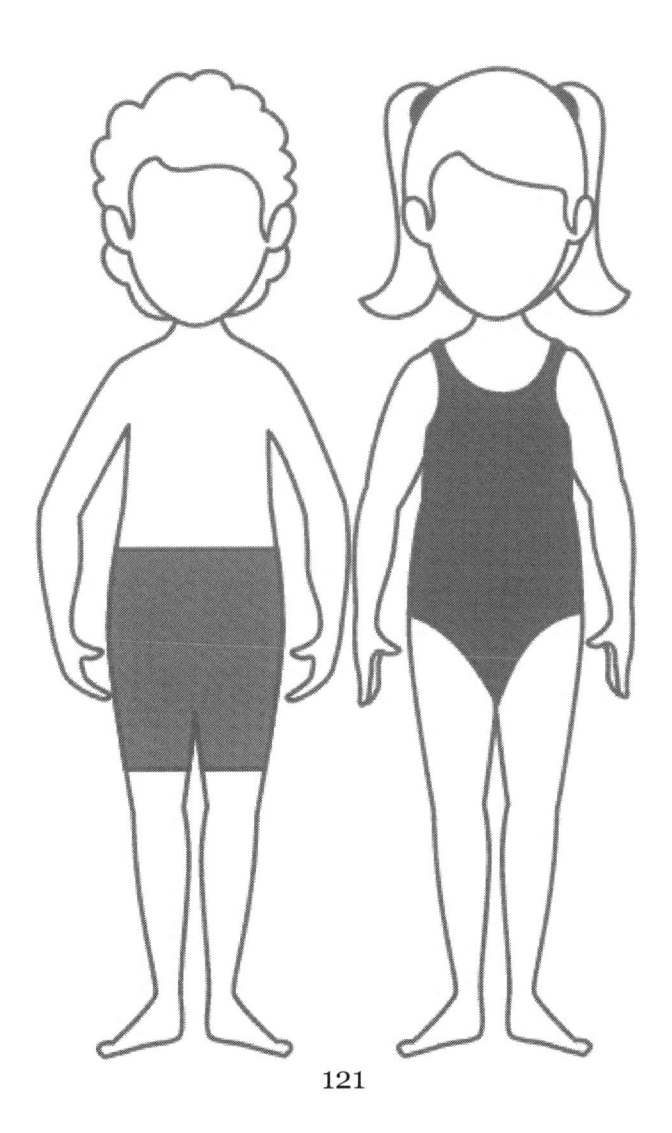

Time Boundaries

Time Boundaries are rules that help you manage your hours and ensure you have enough time for what you want and need to do. They're like setting limits on how long you spend on different activities. Here are some examples of time boundaries:

Time for Fun: It's important to engage in fun activities like playing with your toys, going out with friends, watching cartoons, or going to the park.

Time for Learning: School is important, so there should always be time in your day for learning and schoolwork.

Time for Rest: Your body needs rest, so it's a good idea to carve some alone time or downtime when needed. A sleeping schedule (i.e., going to bed and waking up at the same time each day) also helps you feel refreshed and ready for the day.

Time with Family: Family time, such as eating dinner together, talking, or playing games, is a great way to strengthen family bonds.

Time for Chores: Being part of a family means helping whenever possible. So, set aside some time for chores and helping out at home (e.g., making your bed, setting and clearing the table, watering plants, etc.).

Time for Yourself: You should also have some time just for you. This could be when you read a book, draw, or do something you enjoy alone.

Time boundaries are like a schedule that helps you balance everything you want and need to do. They ensure you have time for fun, learning, rest, and spending time with loved ones. It's all about managing your time wisely!

Worksheet: Boundary O'clock

Imagine your day is divided into hours, just like a clock. Each hour represents different activities or boundaries. Draw or write in the clock below to show how you would spend your day. Be sure to include time for all the important boundaries and activities. Here are some tips:

- Fill in the clock to create your daily schedule.
- Include the time you wake up, go to school, have playtime, eat meals, do homework, do chores, have free time, spend time with your family, and go to bed.
- Make sure to leave some time for yourself to do things you enjoy!

Here's an example:

Now, it's your turn:

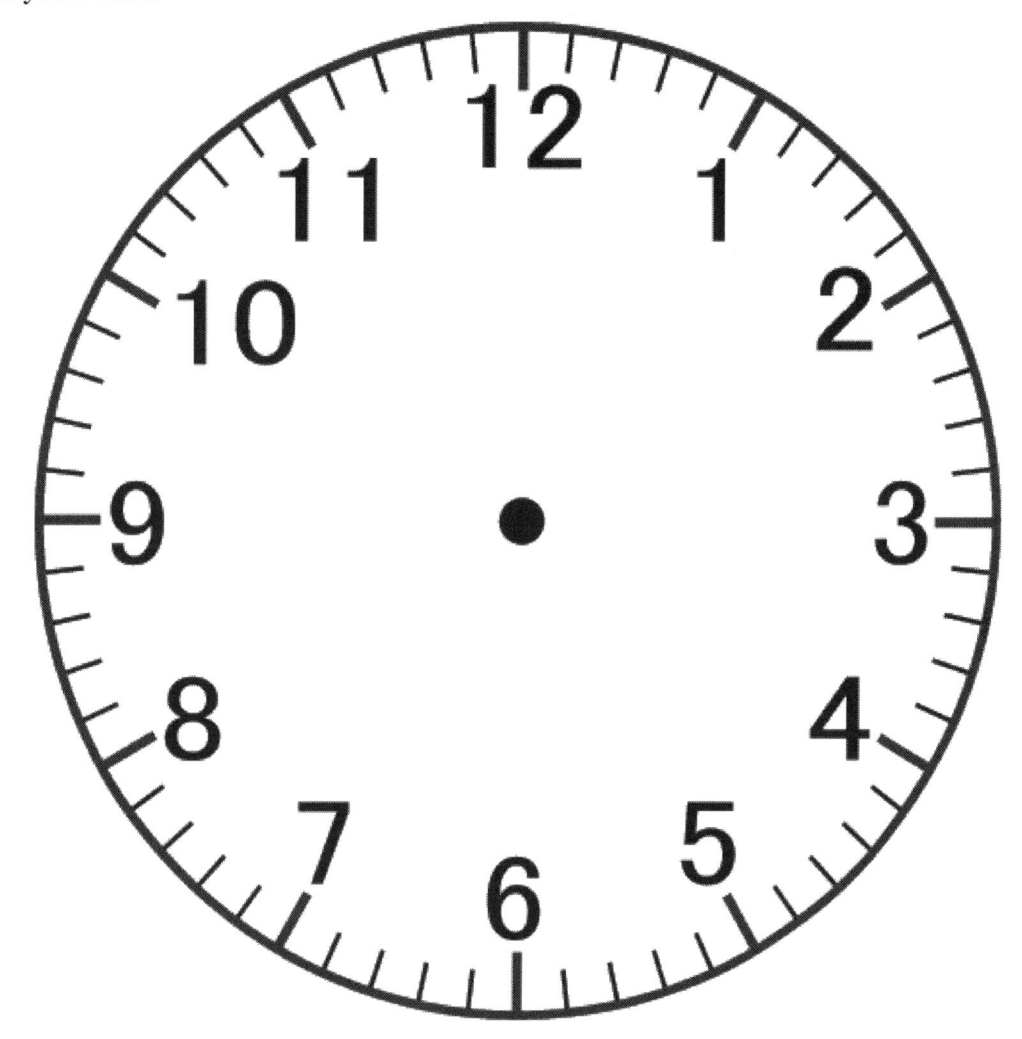

Remember, setting time boundaries helps you have a balanced day!

Online Boundaries and Safety

According to The American Academy of Child Psychiatry (AACP), kids ages 8 to 12 spend an average of 4 to 6 hours a day watching or using screens.[6,7] Now, that's A LOT of screen time.

Sure, you need to be online for school stuff. Still, suppose you stay online for HOURS to watch funny videos, play online games, or look at what other people do on social media (e.g., TikTok, Instagram, YouTube, etc.). In that case, it really isn't very healthy for you.

Imagine your body and mind like a plant. Plants need sunshine, water, and fresh air to grow strong and healthy, right? Well, your body and mind need some special things, too!

You need real-life adventures! Spending too much time online might miss out on things like playing with friends, exploring the outdoors, or reading a fun book. These adventures help you grow and learn in different ways.

You need enough sleep time. Staying up late online can make you tired and grumpy, just like missing sleep can make a plant droop. Your body needs good sleep to stay active and alert during the day.

You need a balanced diet of activities. Just like plants need a balanced diet of water and nutrients, your mind needs to be engaged with plenty of different stuff to develop well. If you're online all the time, you might miss out on other fun things like drawing, playing sports, or learning new skills.

You need REAL friends. While online friends can be great, having real friends is important, too. Spending time together face-to-face helps you build strong and lasting friendships.

Spending time online is okay, but just like a plant needs balance to grow, you need to balance your online time with real-life activities to keep your body and mind healthy and happy.

Online Privacy and Safety

Imagine the internet as one giant playground, and you're playing there. Super fun, right?

When you're on the internet, you do different activities like watching videos, playing games, talking to friends, or looking at fun stuff, right? But, like on a real playground, *other people* can see what you're doing online.

How? Well, imagine your digital screen as a two-way mirror.

On one side of your screen, that's you using the internet. But, on the other side—the side you can't see—some grown-ups and websites might be watching what you're doing. I know, creepy!

This means that when you're online, you must be very careful because some people and websites might want to know things about you, like your name or where you live. Just like you wouldn't want strangers peeking through the two-way mirror to see you in your room, you don't want strangers to know too much about you online. You need to keep some things private when you're online. What things?

1. **Personal Stuff.** Never share your full name, address, phone number, or school with people you meet online. These details enable strangers to find you.

2. **Money Stuff.** Sometimes, you might end up on a website asking for your parent's credit card details or bank information. They might even pretend you won something and just want to know where to send the money. When this happens, don't share anything. Leave the site and tell your parents or a trusted adult about it.

3. **Posting Pictures.** Be careful about the pictures you share online. Don't post pictures that show your home, school, or any information that can identify your location.

4. **Online Games.** If you're playing online games, avoid using your real name as your username. Use a made-up name to protect your identity.

5. **Chatting with Strangers.** If someone you don't know tries to chat with you online, don't share personal information. Tell your parents or an adult you trust if they ask you something that makes you feel uncomfortable.

6. **Friend Requests.** Only accept friend requests from people you know in real life. Sometimes, people pretend to be someone else online.

7. **Email and Messaging.** Be careful when opening emails or messages from unknown people. Don't click on any links or download attachments unless you're sure it's safe.

Using the internet can be fun, just like playing on a real playground. But remember, by keeping some things private and not sharing too much with strangers, you can have a safe and fun time online, just like playing without worries on a playground!

Worksheet: Online Safety Quiz

Let's see how much you know about staying safe online. Answer these questions to test your online safety knowledge.

1. **True or False.** It's okay to share your full name, address, and phone number with someone you meet online.

    ☐ True
    ☐ False

2. **What's the right thing to do?** If a stranger online asks, "What school do you go to?" you should:

    ☐ Tell them the name of your school.
    ☐ Ignore the question.
    ☐ Share your school's name and address.

3. **What's the smart thing to do?** If you get a message from a website that says, "Congratulations! You just won a prize. Please tell us where to send it." you should:

    ☐ Go and get your parent's credit card info and put that in.
    ☐ Share your home address.
    ☐ Ignore the question and leave the website.

4. **Multiple Choice.** When creating an online username, which is the safest choice?

    ☐ Your full name.
    ☐ A nickname or made-up name.
    ☐ Your home address.

5. **True or False.** It's safe to accept friend requests from people you've never met in real life.

   ☐ True
   ☐ False

6. **What should you do?** If someone you don't know online asks for your password, you should.

   ☐ Share it with them.
   ☐ Ignore their request.
   ☐ Ask your parents if you should share it.

7. **True or False.** It's safe to open emails and messages from anyone, even if you don't know the sender.

   ☐ True
   ☐ False

8. **True or False.** You should always check with a trusted adult before downloading anything from the internet.

   ☐ True
   ☐ False

How did you do? Check your answers with a trusted adult to learn more about staying safe online!

Cyberbullying

Cyberbullying is when someone uses their phone, computer, or other devices to say mean things, spread rumors, or hurt others online. It's like when you play a game with your friends, and everyone follows the rules and has fun, but then someone breaks them and tries to make others feel bad or scared.

Imagine if someone sent you mean messages or made fun of you online. That's cyberbullying, and it's NOT okay. It's important to tell a grown-up you trust if it happens to you or if you see it happening to another kid. We all deserve to be treated with kindness and respect, whether playing at the playground or on the internet.

Of course, cyberbullying can be very upsetting. That's why you need to stand up against it because if you don't and someone keeps cyberbullying you, you'll keep feeling sad.

However, there's a RIGHT way to deal with cyberbullies.

How to Deal with Cyberbullies	
Positive Ways	**Negative Ways**
Tell a Trusted Adult: If someone is being mean to you online, tell a grown-up you trust, like your parents or a teacher. They can help you make it stop.	**Keeping It a Secret:** Don't keep cyberbullying a secret. It's important to tell someone you trust, like a grown-up, so they can help.
Block or Unfriend: You can block or unfriend the person being mean to you. This way, they won't be able to bother you anymore.	**Hiding:** Avoiding the internet because of a cyberbully is not a solution. You should be able to enjoy the online world safely. Remember, you deserve a space there too.
Stay Calm: Cyberbullies want to see you upset. They might stop bothering you if you stay calm and don't react.	**Sharing Personal Information:** Don't share personal information, like your address or phone number, with cyberbullies or anyone online.

How to Deal with Cyberbullies	
Positive Ways	**Negative Ways**
Save Evidence: If someone is cyberbullying you, save the messages or pictures as proof. You might need them later to show a grown-up.	**Bullying Back:** It's not a good idea to be mean to cyberbullies in return. It can make things worse and hurt others, too.
Talk to Friends: Share your feelings with friends or a trusted adult. They can offer support and make you feel better.	**Seeking Revenge:** Trying to get back at a cyberbully is not a good idea. It can make the situation worse and get you into trouble.
Report It: On many websites and apps, there is a way to report cyberbullying. Use this feature to let the people who run the website know what's happening.	**Ignoring It Completely:** Ignoring cyberbullying is okay to some extent, but if it continues, it's important to take action and tell a trusted adult.

Remember, it's always best to talk to a grown-up you trust when dealing with cyberbullying. They can help you feel better and find the right way to handle the situation.

As you can see, the online world can be super-duper fun but also an unhealthy, dangerous and scary place! ☹ So, how can you enjoy AND be safe at the same time? That's where online boundaries come into play.

Online Boundaries

Online Boundaries are rules or guidelines that help you have a great time on the internet while keeping you safe and happy. Let's explore some of these online boundaries together so you can be a super-smart and responsible internet explorer!

1. **Set screen time limits.** Your parents can help you decide how much time you should spend online daily. Stick to those limits—for your own good!

2. **Respect screen-free zones**. Are there screen-free zones in your home? If so, this means that your parents or caregivers want these areas (e.g., dining table, living room,

etc.) reserved for other important activities, like eating or spending quality time with family. Respect these zones because they help build a happy family. Plus, these places also give your eyes and brain a break from screens, which is important for your health and sleep.[8]

3. **Always keep personal info private.** As we discussed, don't share your full name, address, phone number, or school with people you meet online.

4. **Use strong passwords.** Protect any online accounts with strong and unique passwords, like your social media stuff. Don't share them with anyone except your parents.

5. **BE KIND ONLINE**. Treat others how you want to be treated. Use kind words and emojis, just like you would in real life.

6. **Think before you share.** Be careful with what you post online. Remember, it can be hard to take back once it's out there.

7. **Ask permission.** Not everything online is fun and safe, so always ask your parents before downloading apps or games and before sharing pictures of yourself with others.

8. **Privacy settings.** Learn how to use the privacy settings of the websites you visit, including social media and any gaming accounts. Using these settings wisely will help you control who can see your information.

9. **DON'T meet anyone you've only talked to online.** People online aren't always who they say they are. So if someone asks you to meet up in person, ALWAYS talk to your parents about it first.

Remember, these boundaries are there to keep you safe from harm. Some may seem annoying, but it's always better to be safe than sorry.

Self-Boundaries

Self-boundaries are rules you make for yourself to stay healthy, happy, and safe. This includes taking the time to take care of yourself.

Taking care of yourself is like making sure you have enough energy and happiness inside you. Imagine that you have a magic cup filled with your happiness and energy. When your cup is full, you feel great and can share your happiness with others. But if you don't care for yourself, your cup gets empty, and you might feel tired or sad. And it's hard to make others happy if you don't have enough happiness inside you to share.

So, taking care of yourself is like filling your magic cup. When its full, you can make yourself and others happy, and that's why it's important!

Taking care of yourself means having some "personal rules" or "ME rules." Just like you have rules at home or school, you can also have rules for yourself! These are called self-boundaries.

A bit confused? No worries; here's a **Self-Boundaries Magic Adventure Map** just for you!

1. **The Super Sleep Sanctuary.** Set a bedtime boundary (what time to go to bed and what time to wake up) to ensure you get enough sleep and feel like a superhero!

2. **The Healthy Snack Spot**. Set a boundary to eat a colorful fruit or veggie daily to keep your magic energy strong.

3. **The Fun Screen Time Trail.** Decide how much time you can spend on screens daily to protect your magic focus and imagination.

4. **The Homework Hideaway.** Create a boundary to finish your homework before you play to become the smartest explorer.

5. **The Toy Treasure Trove.** Share some of your toys with friends or siblings to spread joy and friendship like a magic gift.

6. **The Happy Hobby Haven.** Find a hobby that makes you smile and set aside time to practice it, like painting or playing music.

7. **The Adventure Break Oasis.** Take little breaks to run, jump, or dance during the day so your magic energy stays high.

8. **The Kindness Cove.** Promise to be kind to everyone you meet on your daily journey.

9. **The Super Saver's Secret.** Save a little bit of your allowance or gift money in your treasure chest (i.e., piggy bank or savings jar) to learn about the magic of saving.

10. **The Feel-Good Forest.** Keep a special journal where you write down things that make you happy so you can always find your magic smile.

Taking care of yourself is amazing. It makes you happy, healthy, kind, safe, and other feel-good stuff. But did you know that **asking for help is also a way of caring for yourself**?

Asking for help is like sending a message or special SOS to your fellow adventurers when you need assistance. Like superheroes who work together as a team, you can ask grown-ups or friends for help when you face big challenges.

Here's when you can ask for help:

- When you're sad or scared (like a brave knight might feel when facing a dragon).
- When you're confused or lost (like feeling lost in a maze).
- When you're unsure what to do (like an apprentice asking a wise wizard for advice).

Remember, practicing self-care and asking for help are superpowers that make you an even stronger and happier adventurer!

Worksheet: Self-Care Bingo

Self-care is all about taking time for yourself and feeling good! To play this game, choose any row, column, or diagonal of self-care activities to complete. When you've completed a line, shout "Bingo!" and treat yourself to something special.

SELF-CARE BINGO!

Read a Book: Spend some time reading a book you love or exploring a new one.	**Write in a Journal:** Share your thoughts and feelings in a special journal.	**Dance to Your Favorite Song:** Put on some music and dance like nobody's watching!
Go for a Nature Walk: Take a walk outside and enjoy the fresh air and nature around you.	**Do a Puzzle:** Challenge yourself with a puzzle or brain teaser.	**Take Deep Breaths:** Practice deep breathing to calm your mind and body.
Draw or Color: Get creative with some drawing or coloring.	**Play with a Pet:** Spend quality time with a furry friend.	**Help with Chores:** Do a small chore to feel helpful and skillful.
Call or Video Chat with a Friend: Get in touch with a friend you haven't seen in a while.	**Practice Mindfulness:** Try a mindfulness exercise like mindful breathing, mindful eating, or just staying quiet for 5 minutes to relax and stay present.	**Have a Healthy Snack:** Enjoy a tasty and nutritious treat.

Firm, Fuzzy, and Shifting Boundaries

All boundaries are important. But not all are set in stone; some can be flexible.

Firm or hard boundaries are like strong castle walls that protect something important. There are hardly ever any exceptions to these boundaries. For example, "no hitting each other" might be a hard boundary between yourself, your brothers and sisters, and your classmates. Another example of a hard boundary is "no touching" by strangers on body parts covered by your swimsuit.

Do you have other **firm boundaries** you want to share? Write them down here!

- _____
- _____
- _____
- _____
- _____

Fuzzy boundaries are like doors that are sometimes open and sometimes closed. It's a bit flexible, like saying, "You can come in, but only sometimes." For example, when playing with friends in the playground, you might be okay with a little pushing, pulling, and grabbing. It's all part of playing, right? But if someone starts playing too rough, you might want to "close the door" and establish a boundary. You might say, "Hey, you're pushing too hard. Stop it!"

Do you have other **fuzzy boundaries** you want to share? Write them down here!

- _____
- _____
- _____
- _____
- _____

Shifting boundaries are boundaries that can change depending on the situation. It means you might be okay with something, and then, in the middle of a situation, you might want to change your mind. And that's okay! For example, you feel too old to sit on grandma's lap, but you're still pretty much okay with it. However, suppose grandma tries to feed you cake while sitting on her lap, and you don't want that. In this case, your boundary has shifted from "okay" to "no."

Do you have other **shifting boundaries** you want to share? Write them down here!

- _____
- _____
- _____
- _____
- _____

Remember, having different types of boundaries in different situations is okay, and you can decide what's right for you!

Respect for Others' Boundaries

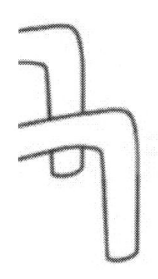

Tibby: Hi! I'm Tibby, and this is my younger brother, Zip.
Lulu: Hi, I'm Lulu, and this is my twin, Marley.
Tibby: So nice to meet you! You know, there's a cool swing on the other side of this playground. Let's go and play together!"
Marley: That sounds like a lot of fun, Tibby, but we're not quite ready to play right now. We want some time to relax and chat first. Maybe next time.
Tibby: Oh, okay. See you around!

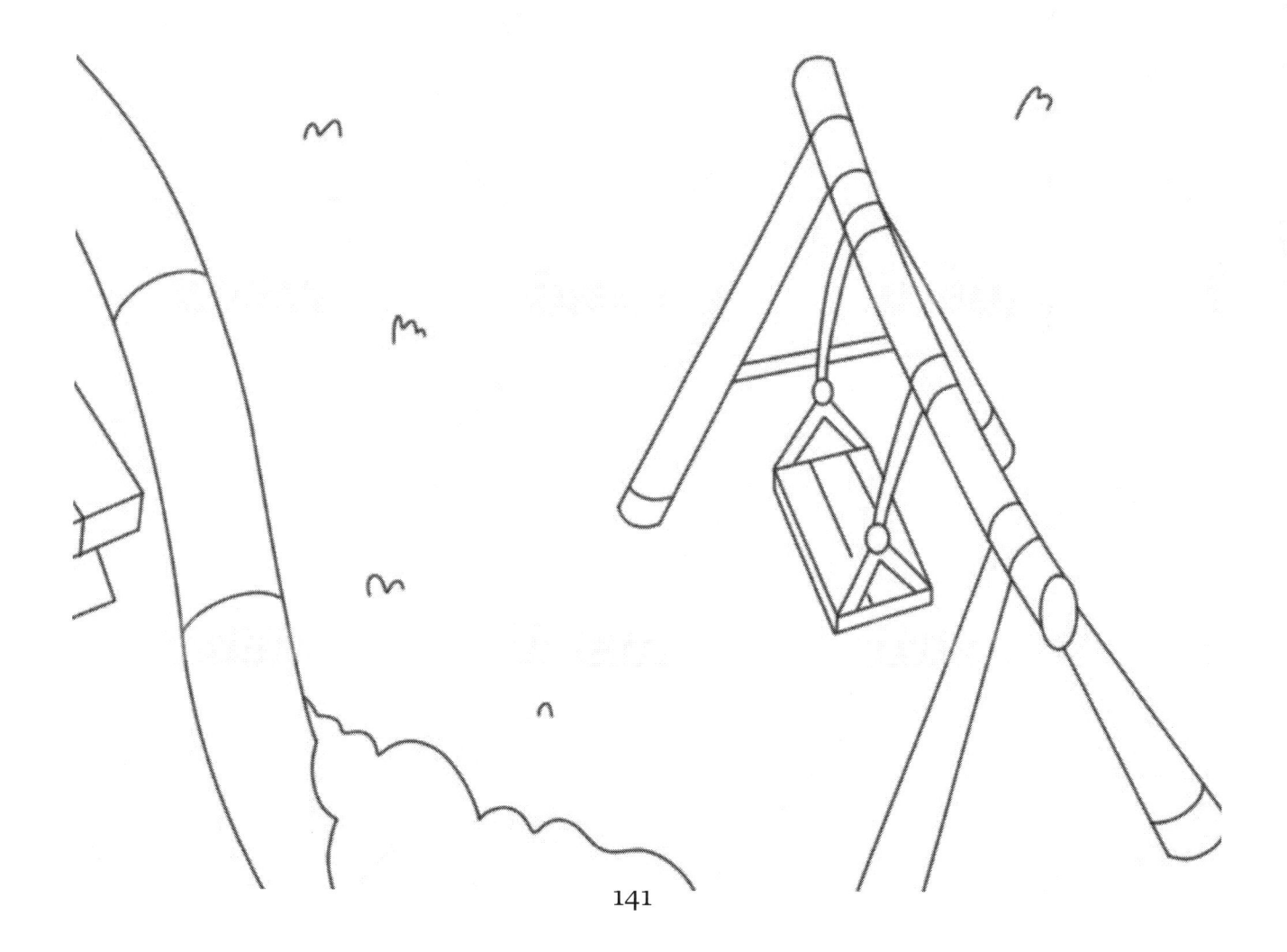

So far, we've talked about your boundaries and their importance for your well-being. But guess what? Just like you have boundaries, other people have them too! And being a great kid means respecting their boundaries.

Now, you might wonder, "How do I know someone else's boundaries?" Sometimes, they're pretty clear about what they like and don't like, but other times, they might not say it out loud but give you little clues and signals instead. It's like a secret code of feelings you can learn to read!

Reading Signs of Discomfort in Others

1. **Facial Expressions.** Watch for frowns, raised eyebrows, or eyes that look worried. These can show that someone is not feeling comfortable.
2. **Body Language.** If someone looks tense, stiff, or trying to move away, they might be uncomfortable.
3. **Not Making Eye Contact.** Sometimes, people avoid looking at you when they're uncomfortable or shy.
4. **Crossed Arms or Legs.** When someone crosses their arms or legs, it can mean they're feeling defensive or closed off.
5. **Backing Away.** If someone steps back or moves away, you might invade their personal space.
6. **Fidgeting.** When people fiddle with their hands, hair, or clothing, it can mean they're nervous or uneasy.
7. **Not Joining In.** If someone doesn't want to play or join a conversation, they might feel uncomfortable at that moment.
8. **Quietness.** When someone suddenly becomes very quiet, it could be because they feel uneasy or upset.
9. **Change in Tone.** Listen to their voice; they might feel uncomfortable if it gets shaky, quiet, or sharp.

Being a good kid means noticing these signs and being kind and respectful. If you see any of the above signs, here's what you can do to make things better.

Say Sorry. If you realize you got too close or made someone uncomfortable, the first thing to do is say sorry. "Sorry" is like a magic word you can use to show you didn't mean to upset them.

Step Back. Give the other person some space right away. It's like taking a step back to show you respect their boundaries.

Ask if they're okay. After apologizing and stepping back, you can ask the person if they're okay. It's like checking if they need help in case they feel upset.

Be kind. Treat the person with kindness and continue playing or talking as friends. A sprinkle of friendship always makes things better!

Learn from what happened. Remember what happened so you can be more careful next time.

Worksheet: Personal Space Invader Detective

Ready to play detective?

Remember our discussion about personal space? It's that invisible bubble around you where you feel comfortable and safe. Sometimes, you may be so focused on protecting your personal space that you may accidentally invade others'. Oops!

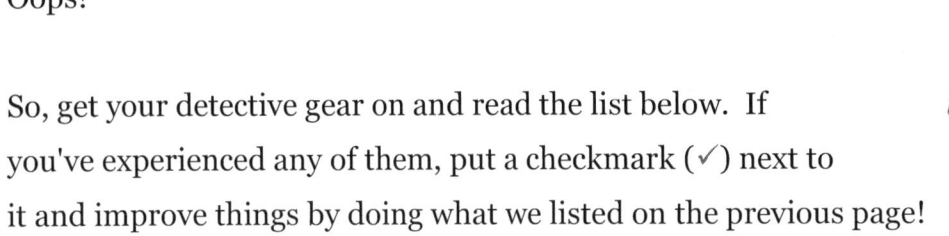

So, get your detective gear on and read the list below. If you've experienced any of them, put a checkmark (✓) next to it and improve things by doing what we listed on the previous page!

- ☐ A person avoids eye contact or starts looking around when you talk to them.
- ☐ A person turns their shoulder away from you.
- ☐ A person's body seems to get stiff when you're around.
- ☐ A person moves around a lot when you are trying to talk to them.
- ☐ A person takes a step back when you move towards them
- ☐ A person changes seats when you sit down next to them.
- ☐ A person starts to close their arms when you talk.
- ☐ A person starts to get squirmy when you are standing or sitting near them.
- ☐ A person's face looks annoyed, worried, confused or uncomfortable.
- ☐ A person abruptly tries to leave when you arrive.
- ☐ A person gives you very short answers when you ask them a question.

Learning to Ask for Permission

Would you enter a magical castle if you hadn't asked permission first? You probably shouldn't because you don't know if any wizards in there would get angry!

Asking for permission is checking with someone *before* doing something. It's a way of showing respect and being polite. And guess what? It also helps you avoid crossing other people's boundaries!

Here's how you can do it:

1. **Say, "May I...".** Start your request with "May I..." like, "May I use your crayons, please?"

2. **Use friendly words.** Always say "please" to show you're being polite. It's like adding a sprinkle of kindness to whatever you're asking.

3. **Listen and respect their answer.** If the person says "yes," that's great! If they say "no," respect their decision and say, "Oh, okay."

4. **Wait for your turn.** If someone is using or doing something, wait patiently for your turn to ask.

Remember, asking for permission is a superpower that helps you build strong relationships and show respect for others' things and feelings.

Conclusion

Boundaries are SUPER IMPORTANT. They protect you from unpleasant feelings (e.g., sadness, fear, anger, etc.) and keep you from danger and harm.

Sometimes, things go wrong because you don't know your boundaries. For example, if you don't set a self-boundary about what time you should go to sleep, you might stay up playing, and then you won't have enough energy for tomorrow. Here's another example: if you don't establish a boundary about your personal space, people will keep crossing it. This might make you feel constantly annoyed, angry, or even afraid.

Although there are many different types of boundaries (family, friends, feelings, online, etc.), it's not hard to figure out what they are. Just ask yourself questions like:

What do I like?
What don't I like?
What makes me feel safe?
Who makes me uncomfortable?

So, the first step is to KNOW your boundaries. After you identify them, it's important to tell others about them because boundaries are not secrets you keep; they are guidelines to live by and communicate to others. When you let others know your boundaries, you're helping them understand how to treat you nicely, respectfully, and kindly.

But you have to remember that other people have boundaries, too! And it would be best if you respected theirs.

So, dear boundary explorers, we hope this boundary journey has been enlightening and empowering. Remember, boundaries are like your trusty compass in life, guiding you toward safety, respect, and healthy relationships.

As you grow and face new adventures, always carry the wisdom of setting and respecting boundaries with you. Whether it's your personal space, emotions, or precious dreams, know they are worth protecting and sharing wisely.

Bonus Section for Parents or Caregivers: How to Help Your Child Set Boundaries

Raising kids, especially in today's world, is exciting and nerve-wracking. But as much as you want to be there always by their side, you can't. This is why you must teach them about boundaries because these are their shields or invisible protective gear wherever they are.

But let's pause for a moment and turn the spotlight on YOU. How are your boundaries doing? It's common for many adults to overlook self-care[9,10], which often goes hand in hand with neglecting to identify and assert boundaries.

So, perhaps the initial step in teaching kids about boundaries begins with some self-reflection. Take a short break, find a quiet moment, and treat yourself to a soothing cup of coffee or tea. Spend a few minutes in introspection. Consider the boundaries you've established (or haven't), the limits you've set (or haven't), and whether some individuals or situations require some boundary reinforcement. You'll feel rejuvenated after giving yourself this well-deserved time!

Another reason you might want to reflect on your boundaries is because you want to lead by example. Kids are smart, and they learn just by observing you. Besides, they're more likely to heed your teachings about boundaries if they see you heeding yours.

So, now that we've got that covered, here are some tips to help you help your child figure out their boundaries.

Discuss things openly. When discussing boundaries, let your child freely voice out what they like and don't like, what makes them happy, what bothers them, and so on. You can guide them with their boundaries later. For now, just let them talk. Create a safe space where they feel comfortable discussing their boundaries and concerns.

Emphasize that boundaries are like shields of protection. A child might not want to set or enforce boundaries because they don't want to offend anyone; i.e., they don't want anyone to get mad at them. Explain that boundaries are not intended to offend other people but rather to protect themselves from being upset or in danger.

Discuss different types of boundaries. Explain to your child that there are different types of boundaries, including physical, emotional, social, online, etc. If they get confused, go back to basics and ask simple questions like, "Is that okay with you?" "Why did that make you upset?" etc.

Also, use age-appropriate examples so your child easily understands what you're trying to say.

Make it fun! Make discussing and setting boundaries fun by creating something like a *Boundary Manifesto* or *[Child's Name] Boundary Rules*. Get whatever supplies you need and create a big poster listing their boundaries AND the consequences of crossing them. Hang it up as a visual reminder for everyone.

Commemorate the moment. Honor the moment you discussed boundaries by creating a boundary bracelet together, gifting your child a boundary journal, or anything you want to commemorate the moment AND to remind your child to uphold their boundaries.

Respect their boundaries. Once they've communicated their boundaries, you must respect them. For example, say that your child doesn't like grandma and grandpa kissing them. Respect this, and don't tell them to make an exception. You can offer alternatives, though. For example, ask them if they're comfortable with a hug instead of a kiss. If not, ask them what *they* think is a good alternative. Let them provide the solutions. It will be a great problem-solving exercise for them.

Take their boundaries seriously. A child's feelings are easily bruised, so don't brush off boundaries they've communicated to you. For example, if they say they don't like being kissed in front of all their friends when you drop them off at school, don't say something like, "Oh, come on. What's one little kiss from your mom/dad."

Use role-playing. Engage in role-playing scenarios to help your child practice setting boundaries and handling situations where their boundaries are crossed. For example, many kids might be shy or afraid to say "No" to someone of authority. Help them by role-playing sample situations at home so they can get used to saying "No."

Role-playing encourages your child to set boundaries and might prevent a bad situation from worsening. For example, suppose someone is pulling your child's hair at school. They're upset, but they're putting up with the bullying. One day, they just can't take it anymore, so they shove the other kid to the ground and hit them with a heavy book, causing the other to bleed. Role-playing may help prevent such a situation.

Teach them what to do when their boundaries get crossed. It's important to teach your child what to do if someone disregards their boundaries. Pre-discuss what to do with "first-time offenders" and "repeat offenders,"
situations when they should get a grown-up immediately, etc.

Give your child a pat on the back! Celebrate your child's efforts in setting and maintaining boundaries. For example, if your child comes home with tales of how they enforced a boundary, congratulate them, say dessert is in their honor, or set a weekend date with them.

Remind them of the "golden rule." Teach your child to respect the boundaries of others, whether it's their friends, classmates, or family members. Remind them of the golden rule: treat others as you would like to be treated.

Helping your child set boundaries is an ongoing process. But with patience and providing guidance, encouragement, and a safe space for open communication, you can empower your child to set and maintain healthy boundaries for their happiness, safety, and protection.

Review Request

If you enjoyed this book or found it useful...

I'd like to ask you for a quick favor:

Please share your thoughts and leave a quick REVIEW. Your feedback matters and helps me make improvements to provide the best books possible.

Reviews are so helpful to both readers and authors, so any help would be greatly appreciated. You can leave a review here:

https://tinyurl.com/Boundaries-for-Kids-Review

Or by scanning the QR code below:

Also, please join my ARC team to get early access to my releases.

https://barretthuang.com/arc-team/

Thank you!

Further Reading
DBT Workbook for Kids

Fun & Practical Dialectal Behavior Therapy Skills Training For Children

Help Kids Recognize Their Emotions, Manage Anxiety & Phobias, and Learn To Thrive!

Get your copy here:

https://tinyurl.com/dbtkids

DBT Workbook For Teens

A Complete Dialectical Behavior Therapy Toolkit

Essential Coping Skills and Practical Activities To Help Teenagers & Adolescents Manage Stress, Anxiety, ADHD, Phobias & More

Get your copy here:

https://tinyurl.com/dbt-teens

About the Author

Barrett Huang is an author and businessman. Barrett spent years discovering the best ways to manage his OCD, overcome his anxiety, and learn to embrace life. Through his writing, he hopes to share his knowledge with readers, empowering people of all backgrounds with the tools and strategies they need to improve their mental wellbeing and be happy and healthy.

When not writing or running his business, Barrett loves to spend his time studying. He has majored in psychology and completed the DBT skills certificate course by Dr. Marsha Linehan. Barrett's idol is Bruce Lee, who said, "The key to immortality is first living a life worth remembering."

https://barretthuang.com/

References

1 Rideout, V., Peebles, A., Mann, S., & Robb, M. B. (2022). The Common Sense Census: Media Use by Tweens and Teens. San Francisco, CA; Common Sense.

2 Paruthi, S., Brooks, L. J., D'Ambrosio, C., Hall, W. A., Kotagal, S., Lloyd, R. M., Malow, B. A., Maski, K., Nichols, C., Quan, S. F., Rosen, C. L., Troester, M. M., & Wise, M. S. (2016). Consensus statement of the American Academy of Sleep Medicine on the recommended amount of sleep for Healthy Children: Methodology and discussion. *Journal of Clinical Sleep Medicine*, *12*(11), 1549–1561. https://doi.org/10.5664/jcsm.6288

3 Mohan, A., Sen, P., Peeush, P., Shah, C., & Jain, E. (2022). Impact of online classes and home confinement on myopia progression in children during COVID-19 pandemic: Digital Eye Strain Among Kids (desk) study 4. *Indian Journal of Ophthalmology*, *70*(1), 241. https://doi.org/10.4103/ijo.ijo_1721_21

4 Gasser, C. E., Mensah, F. K., Russell, M., Dunn, S. E., & Wake, M. (2016). Confectionery consumption and overweight, obesity, and related outcomes in children and adolescents: A systematic review and meta-analysis. *The American Journal of Clinical Nutrition*, *103*(5), 1344–1356. https://doi.org/10.3945/ajcn.115.119883

5 Strasburger, V. C., Hogan, M. J., Mulligan, D. A., Ameenuddin, N., Christakis, D. A., Cross, C., Fagbuyi, D. B., Hill, D. L., Levine, A. E., McCarthy, C., Moreno, M. A., & Swanson, W. S. (2013). Children, adolescents, and the media. *Pediatrics*, *132*(5), 958–961. https://doi.org/10.1542/peds.2013-2656

6 Centers for Disease Control and Prevention. (2018, January 29). *Infographics - screen time vs. Lean Time*. Centers for Disease Control and Prevention. https://www.cdc.gov/nccdphp/dnpao/multimedia/infographics/getmoving.html

7 Naik, A. (2023, March 17). *Screen Time for Kids: How much is too much?*. GoHenry. https://www.gohenry.com/us/blog/parental-controls/screen-time-for-kids-how-much-is-too-much

8 Stiglic, N., & Viner, R. M. (2019). Effects of screentime on the health and well-being of children and adolescents: A systematic review of reviews. *BMJ Open*, *9*(1). https://doi.org/10.1136/bmjopen-2018-023191

9 Aswell, S. (2019, June 24). *New Study finds moms feel guilty for taking time for self care*. Scary Mommy. https://www.scarymommy.com/birchbox-study-self-care Updated: June 8, 2020

10 Parks, E. (2021, December 22). *5 reasons we don't take care of ourselves*. Psychology Today. https://www.psychologytoday.com/us/blog/pain-rehabilitation/202112/5-reasons-we-don-t-take-care-ourselves
Reviewed by Abigail Fagan

Made in United States
Troutdale, OR
04/16/2025